The Power of Consciousness
and the Force of Circumstances
in Sartre's Philosophy

John Sallis, general editor

Consulting Editors

The Power of Consciousness and the Force of Circumstances in Sartre's Philosophy

Thomas W. Busch

Indiana
University
Press

Bloomington and Indianapolis

Manufactured in the United States of America

Library of Congress Cataloging-in-Publication Data

Busch, Thomas
The power of consciousness and the force of
circumstances in Sartre's philosophy.

(Studies in continental thought)
Bibliography: p.
Includes index.
1. Sartre, Jean Paul, 1905–   . I. Title.
II. Series.
B2430.S34B87 1990   194   89-45191
ISBN 0-253-31283-3

1 2 3 4 5   94 93 92 91 90

for
Nancy Hughes Busch

CONTENTS

Abbreviations of Works of Jean-Paul Sartre

TE	*The Transcendence of the Ego,* tr. of *La Transcendance de l'ego* (1936) by Forrest Williams and Robert Kirkpatrick. New York: Noonday Press, 1957.
CF	"Cartesian Freedom," tr. of "La liberté cartésienne" (1945) by Annette Michelson. In *Literary and Philosophical Essays.* New York: Collier Books, 1962.
BN	*Being and Nothingness,* tr. of *L'Être et le Néant* (1943) by Hazel Barnes. New York: Philosophical Library, 1956.
W	*The Words,* tr. of *Les Mots* (1963) by Bernard Frechtman. New York: Fawcett, 1966.
LTM	"Introduction to *Les Temps Modernes,*" tr. of "Présentation des *Temps Modernes,*" (1945) by Françoise Ehrmann. In *Paths to the Present: Aspects of European Thought from Romanticism to Existentialism,* ed. Eugen Weber. New York: Dodd, Mead and Co., 1960.
CP	*The Communists and Peace,* tr. of *Les Communistes et la Paix* (1952) by Martha Fletcher and John Kleinschmidt. New York: Braziller and Co., 1968.
SG	*Saint Genet: Actor and Martyr,* tr. of *Saint Genet, Comédien et Martyr* (1952) by Bernard Frechtman. New York: Mentor, 1963.
SM	*Search for a Method,* tr. of *Questions de méthode* (1957) by Hazel Barnes. New York: Random House, 1958.
CDR I	*Critique of Dialectical Reason,* vol. I, tr. of *Critique de la raison dialectique,* tome I (1960) by Alan Sheridan-Smith. London: Humanities Press, 1976.
CDR II	*Critique de la raison dialectique,* tome II. Paris: Gallimard, 1985. Translations are my own.
C	*Cahiers pour une morale.* Paris: Gallimard, 1983. Translations are my own.
FI I	*The Family Idiot,* vols. 1 and 2, tr. of *L'Idiot de la famille: Gustave*
FI II	*Flaubert de 1821 à 1857,* libre I (1971) by Carol Cosman. Chicago: University of Chicago Press, 1981; 1987.
IF 2	*L'Idiot de la famille,* livre II, Paris: Gallimard, 1971. Translations, unless otherwise indicated, are my own.
WD	*The War Diaries of Jean-Paul Sartre,* tr. of *Les Carnets de la drôle de guerre: Novembre 1939–Mars 1940* (1983) by Quintan Hoare. New York: Pantheon Books, 1984.
BEMIT	"The Itinerary of a Thought," in *Between Existentialism and*

Marxism. Tr. John Matthews. New York: William Morrow and Co., 1974.

SP-L/S "Self-Portrait at Seventy," tr. of "Autoportrait à soixante-dix ans" (1976) by Paul Auster and Lydia Davis. In *Life/Situations: Essays Written and Spoken.* New York: Pantheon Books, 1977.

IF-L/S "On *The Idiot of the Family*," tr. of "Sur *L'Idiot de la famille*" (1976) in *Life/Situations.*

SBH *Sartre by Himself,* tr. of *Sartre: Un filme realisé par Alexandre Astruc et Michel Contat* (1977) by Richard Seaver. New York: Urizen Books, 1978.

A *Adieu: A Farewell to Sartre,* tr. of Simone de Beauvoir's *La Cérémonie des adieux* (1981) by Patrick O'Brien. New York: Pantheon Books, 1984.

O "Jean-Paul Sartre et M. Sicard: Entretien," *Obliques* 18–19 (1979). Translations are my own.

NO "The Last Words of Jean-Paul Sartre," tr. of an interview between Benny Levi and Sartre in *Le Nouvel Observateur,* March 10, 17, and 24, 1980. In *Dissent* (Fall, 1980).

Full information on original French works is given in the bibliography.

For the sake of readability and consistency, minor alterations have been made to several of the English translations.

Introduction

In the film *Sartre by Himself,* Michel Contat asked Jean-Paul Sartre if he ever looked back upon the approximately thirty volumes of his works in order "to seize what unifying thread there is throughout." Sartre replied: "I have gone back to my earlier work, of course, but not so much to try and look for its unity as to re-read some passage out of a previous work. And as for the question of unity, I think there is one but I can't say I've ever tried to look for it. I've never tried to establish it. I think that's a task for other people" (*SBH,* 57). On the same topic, earlier in the film, Sartre had claimed that philosophy is the "unifying element of everything I do, that is, if you like, the only unity there can be among all the different books I've written at a given time is the philosophical unity" (*SBH,* 28). In terms of philosophy it would appear that for Sartre freedom would be the obvious unifying concept, but even on that subject Sartre admitted that he had considerably changed his understanding. In what sense did Sartre's thought change over the course of some fifty years, and in what sense, if at all, does it harbor a unifying thread? This general question of unity marks this study's place of entry into Sartre's works. More specifically, it installs itself within Sartre's thought by defining and tracking down a problematic at its heart, where dominant conceptual strands converge and call one another into question. The problematic forms around the encounter between Sartre's phenomenological existentialism, a synthesis reflected in its maturity in *Being and Nothingness,* and the forms of social alienation subsequently discovered and probed in his writings from *Saint Genet* to *The Family Idiot.* An alternate title might well be "From Project to Totalization," which suggests both a development in Sartre's thought and a change of discourse through which that development is best understood.

The book first explores Sartre's phenomenological existentialism as the expression of the thesis of the power of consciousness, inspired by Cartesian doubt and Husserlian epoché. Chapter 1, "Self," traces the initial formation of Sartre's philosophical discourse from his encounter with Husserl's phenomenology, specifically *Ideas I,* and his translation of its key terms—intentionality, epoché, natural attitude—into a theory of existence whose centerpiece is the notion of the unconditioned project. Chapter 2, "Self/Other," examines *Being and Nothingness* as a theory of reflection and being based upon the subject/object, self/other bifurcations employed to defend the autonomy of the unconditioned project. The book next takes up the relationship between the thesis of the power of consciousness and Sartre's discovery after World War II of *la force des choses*—the power of circumstances. Chapter 3, "The Intrusion of Otherness," examines those postwar works that reflect Sartre's growing awareness of social alienation and solidarity. Chapter 4, "Mediations," explores those later works—*Search for a Method, Critique of Dialectical Reason* I, *The Family Idiot*—that forge concepts to deal with these phenomena. Chapters 3 and 4 reveal the tension and the growing opposition between the fundamental categories of the early works and the late ones. Chapter 5, "Transformation," takes up the notion of totalization, found in its most mature form in *The Family Idiot*, as Sartre's definitive move beyond the earlier notion of project. Totalization recasts the understanding of freedom, recognizes the radical social nature of existence and thought, and is the model that discloses comprehensibly a "unifying thread" throughout Sartre's works. Interviews given by Sartre shortly before he died, particularly the controversial series with Benny Levy in *Le Nouvel Observateur*, which "horrified" Simone de Beauvoir and were "highly significant" to Emmanuel Levinas, are drawn upon to confirm the transformation that took place in Sartre's thought from the time he encountered and tried to make sense of *la force des choses*.

For a long period of his life, Jean-Paul Sartre dreamed of immortality. He hoped to succeed by transforming himself from mere flesh and bones into parchment, cardboard, and leather. He would then be found in the National Library where he would "sit in state through a hundred thirty pounds of paper. . . . Hands take me down, open me, spread me flat on the table, smooth me and sometimes make me creak. I let them, and then suddenly I flash, I dazzle. . . . No one can forget or ignore me" (W, 121–122). As his unpublished works continue to appear—*War Diaries, Cahiers pour une morale, Critique de la Raison Dialectique*, volume II, *Freud Scenario*—the issue of weight is being resolved. During the decades of his activities, Sartre did dazzle, and he could not be ignored. As for the future? He could not, he tells us in *The Words*, think of the "cooling of the sun" without fear, yet before he died he experienced a cooling of interest in his works on the part of the public, particularly the young people whose attention he had always sought. In an interview he gave in May 1975,[1] it was brought to his attention that "many people today are trying to go beyond Sartre without going through Sartre's thought." His response is recorded simply and without further interpretive comment as "Ha-ha!" In another interview the same spring he was asked: "Are you sorry that young intellectuals don't read you any more, that they know you only through false ideas of you and your works?"

Sartre: I would say it's too bad for me.

Interviewer: For you, or for them?

Sartre: To tell the truth, for them too. But I think it is just a passing stage.

Interviewer: Basically you would agree with the prediction Roland Barthes made recently when he said that you will soon be rediscovered and that this will take place soon in a completely natural way?

Sartre: I hope so. (L/S, 23–24)

By this time Sartre had disclaimed any aspiration to immortality, only to yearn for an even more improbable goal, to exist simply as a man among men. An institution in his own time (witness his funeral) he stood out as its conscience, often its judge, addressing issues both perennial and timely, creating a body of work of such quantity and quality that it would be impossible to assess our century without him. Shortly after his death, Michel Rybalka wrote:

> It is too early to evaluate Sartre's place in history and culture. The Sartreans themselves have so far remained silent. That his place is considerable is beyond doubt: Sartre's written work and his political actions are inseparable from what has happened in the last fifty years. As Audiberti termed it, Sartre was present in "all the battlefields of intelligence," and as François Mauriac recognized it, thirty years ago, he is certainly "le contemporain capital." It is for us to see how much Sartre's work and example constitute a hope for the future. As Roland Barthes, who met his untimely death in March, put it: "Sartre est un auteur d'avenir." For the time being, Sartre's death leaves us with a great void.[2]

In terms of the example of his life, his relentless quest to unmask injustice, to speak for the voiceless, to raise the conscience of his fellow citizens, and the price he paid for this, I am convinced that Sartre does constitute a hope for the future. As for his works, we have observed Barthes's forecast of a "rediscovery." Five years after Sartre's death, his biographer Annie Cohen-Solal found that "his work was still alive with a rhythm all its own, unpredictable, headstrong."[3] More recently, Ronald Aronson has observed a "Sartre revival . . . upon us already,"[4] due principally to the richness of the works that have appeared since his death. This is evidence, to be sure, of the vital pulse of Sartre's ideas, but it remains to be seen to what extent those works will be a life-giving transfusion for the future. Sartre's philosophy has been, from the beginning, much misunderstood. Forty-five years after its publication, *Being and Nothingness* is still misread. I will be pleased if this book erases some of these false notions and encourages the fuller appreciation and future reappropriation of Sartre's work.

I am deeply indebted to a number of people who in one way or another have contributed to the realization of this project. My colleague John Caputo has offered continuous encouragement and advice. Thomas R. Flynn furnished many helpful suggestions on the original manuscript. Reverend Lawrence Gallen, O.S.A., Vice-President for Academic Affairs, Villanova University, awarded me a sabbatical leave to complete the manuscript. Sandy Shupard expertly and tirelessly typed the manuscript. Mary Jane Gormley provided invaluable editorial assistance. I am especially grateful to those colleagues in the field of Sartre studies from whom I have learned and by whom I have been inspired and challenged. I acknowledge them in the bibliography, while claiming as my own all of the shortcomings of this book. I am grateful to John Sallis, editor of *Research in Phenomenology*, for permission to use material from my article "Phenomenology and Humanism: The Case of Husserl and Sartre," XI (1979), in chapter one. Finally, my thanks to my wife Nancy for her support, and to my children Caitlin, Cecily, and Aidan, who put up with me while I worked on this project.

The Power of Consciousness
and the Force of Circumstances
in Sartre's Philosophy

ONE

Self

There appeared in 1946 a slim volume of selected texts from René Descartes's works, introduced by Jean-Paul Sartre. The introduction, "Cartesian Freedom," was subsequently reproduced in *Situations I*.[1] This was a unique venture for Sartre, an obvious act of homage to the only Frenchman he claimed to have had a profound influence upon him. Throughout this piece Sartre plays on the theme that it was Descartes who first introduced the notion of an "autonomous thinking," whose essence consists in the power of "refusal" that resides in the heart of methodic doubt. Doubt implies the "power of escaping, disengaging oneself and withdrawing" (*CF*, 190), and is the basis of humanism: "Doubt is a breaking of contact with being. Through doubt, man has a permanent possibility of disentangling himself from the existing universe and of suddenly contemplating it from above as a pure succession of phantasms. In this sense, it is the most magnificent affirmation of the reign of the human" (*CF*, 190). Authoritative forms of givenness, including the evidence of the senses and cultural tradition, are put in abeyance by the power of thought. Consciousness can always "withhold assent," can always "say yes or no." This liberty of indifference implies "negativity" and "no one before Descartes had stressed the connection between free will and negativity" (*CF*, 191). Yet Sartre notes a tension in Descartes's writings between on the one hand the proposal of a methodology of inquiry, a selection of man-made ground rules, and on the other hand a universe whose intelligibility is fixed and imposed by God. While divine and human freedom are the same in the infinity of power of indifference, they differ in creative power.

> Descartes realized perfectly that the concept of freedom involved necessarily an absolute autonomy, that a free act was an absolutely new production, the germ of which could not be contained in an earlier state of the world and that consequently freedom and creation were one and the same. The freedom of God, though similar to that of man, loses the negative aspect that it had in its human envelope; it is pure productivity. (*CF*, 195)

Sartre's claim is that Descartes, in describing God's freedom, was only developing "the implicit content of the idea of freedom," evident in Descartes's "primary intuition of his own freedom" (*CF*, 196). Descartes's failure

1

to grant to human beings the full implication of freedom is seen by Sartre to involve a naiveté about the given order: "he was forced by the age in which he lived . . . to reduce the human free will to a merely negative power to deny itself until it finally yields and abandons itself to the divine solicitude" (*CF*, 196). In an abrupt change of discourse from autonomy to heteronomy the experience of the force of circumstances makes its appearance. The reader has been advised in the discourse of autonomy that through doubt "man has a permanent possibility of disentangling himself from the existing universe and of suddenly contemplating it from above as a pure succession of phantasms" and thus might wonder, given the power of consciousness, how the autonomous thinker could be a victim of his or her given situation. The discourse and metaphors of the power of consciousness are *escape, break, withdrawal, disengagement, disentangling.* No contrasting discourse of the force of circumstances, of victimization, appears. At this time (1946), Sartre had not developed such a discourse, but, as we shall see, was becoming increasingly aware of the need to develop one.

This homage to Descartes as a proto-existentialist admirably expresses Sartre's commitment to the thesis of the power of consciousness. It would be misleading, however, to overestimate Descartes's influence on the development of Sartre's existentialism. When Sartre's friend Jean Pouillon asked him in the film *Sartre by Himself* about his intellectual development, he confronted him with the question, "was the real discovery, in terms of importance to you, [Edmund] Husserl?," Sartre replied, "yes . . . you're quite right; it was Husserl. That's why, when Aron said to me, 'Why, we can reason about this glass of beer. . . .' Simone de Beauvoir immediately interjected herself into the conversion: 'It wasn't a glass of beer. It was an apricot cocktail' [laughter]" (*SBH*, 25). The details of Sartre's encounter with his former classmate and friend, Raymond Aron, in a Paris café in 1932 are recounted for us in de Beauvoir's memoirs. Aron was just visiting Paris at the time; he was on a fellowship that year at the French Institute in Berlin. He had heard of phenomenology and told Sartre that a phenomenologist could "talk about this cocktail and make philosophy out of it." Sartre was excited about the possibility that phenomenology was just the method he was looking for to overcome the antinomies of idealism and realism, so at Aron's suggestion he made arrangements to succeed him in the fellowship for the next year.

When this occurred Sartre was twenty-seven, had received his *agrégation*—with highest honors—in philosophy in 1929, and was teaching philosophy in Le Havre. He was the product of an academic system that, as Colette Audry remarks, scarcely changed in the teaching of philosophy from 1890 to 1930—"obstinately Cartesian and Neo-Kantian, it continued to transmit a rationalistic idealism."[2] From time to time both in his writings and in interviews Sartre commented on his university education. He referred to his teachers on various occasions as "futile and serious," "new Eleatics," and "dreamers." Put off by their idealism and positivism, for his earliest writings he borrowed here and there from the works of Descartes, Immanuel Kant, and Henri Bergson, but as Annie Cohen-Solal remarks, "without recognizing himself in any of them, unable to sympathize. He has no master, no mentor."[3] Educated in an historical era that he later came to define in terms of Marxism, Sartre noted with bitterness that he was not introduced to dialectical thought in the university: "In 1925, when I was twenty years old, there was no chair of Marxism at the University, and Communist students were careful not to appeal to Marxism or even to mention it in their examinations; had they done so, they would have failed. The horror of dialectic was such that [G. W.] Hegel himself was unknown to us" (*SM*, 17). He quoted his teacher Jules Lachelier: "There won't be any Hegel as long as I'm around," and claimed that another teacher, Léon Brunschwicg, in his *La Conscience occidentale*, "devoted no more than a few pages to Hegel, and not a word about Marx" (*SBH*, p. 25). At the *École Normale Supérieure*, Sartre's close friend, the Marxist Paul Nixon, passionately denounced the bourgeois French educational system in 1925. (In 1968, Sartre reiterated his friend's condemnations, wholeheartedly embracing the demands of the student protestors for a thorough change in the educational system.)

Sartre's complaints must be put in perspective; they issued from hindsight. It was not as though he felt a need for the dialectic of Hegel or Marx during his university days. At the beginning of the 1930s an intense interest in Hegel arose in France, generating valuable Hegelian scholarship, but Sartre was not at all an active participant. Rather, he read some Hegel on his own and relied heavily on commentaries; he selectively employed Hegelian concepts, adapted to his purposes, in *Being and Nothingness,* which he was preparing in the late 1930s. Preoccupation with Hegel and Marx—with historical thought—would come only after the war and occupation, precipitated by his growing awareness of the force of circumstances. At the time of his meeting with Aron, Sartre was concerned with psychology, not with history or social phenomena. His project in Berlin was to study "the relationship between the psychic and the physiological." Looking back to this period of his career, in the interview "The Itinerary of a Thought," he recollected that his "preoccupations at the time . . . were at bottom to provide a philosophic foundation for realism . . . which I have tried to do all my life. In other words, how to give man both his autonomy and his reality among real objects, avoiding idealism without lapsing into a mechanistic determinism" (*BEMIT*, 37). As Simone de Beauvoir has remarked, prior to his encounter with phenomenology Sartre's thought lacked a "coherent organization."[4] Whatever creative insights Sartre might have had about contingency and freedom, it was phenomenology that provided a paradigm and language for developing his ideas. In the process Sartre was to shape phenomenology, as it was to shape him.

In 1933, then, Sartre headed for Berlin to pick up "intentionality, situation, and twenty other tools which could be procured in Germany."[5] By this time Edmund Husserl, the founder of transcendental phenomenology, had been in retirement from teaching for several years and resided in Freiburg. Sartre did not study phenomenology under Husserl, but, as he had done with Hegel, read and studied on his own. In regard to his reading of Husserl, Sartre gives evidence of acquaintance with only a few works, principally *Ideas Pertaining to a Pure Phenomenology and to a Phenomenological Philosophy.*

His friend Pouillon asked him, "And in what order did you read Husserl, first the *Ideen,* or did you start with *Logische Untersuchungen?*" Sartre replied "*Ideen,* and nothing but *Ideen.* For me, you know, who don't read very fast, a year was just about right for reading his *Ideen*" (*SBH,* 29–30). His enthusiasm for phenomenology is apparent in a brief article he wrote during his stay in Berlin, "Intentionality: A Fundamental Idea of Husserl's Phenomenology."[6] Husserl and the phenomenologists would finally liberate philosophy from sterile epistemological haggling. The world need not be assimilated to consciousness, nor consciousness to the world: "Consciousness and the world are given simultaneously: external by nature to consciousness, the world is also by nature related to it."[7] Sartre's enthusiasm focused upon what he saw to be phenomenology's realism, its rejection of the model of consciousness as a self-contained immanence "closeted off all warm and cozy." In its favor, phenomenology offered a consciousness that was outside of itself, always in touch with things, but never itself reduced to a thing. Through phenomenology philosophy could be rescued from the abstractions of academics and "thrown headlong into the streets, the city, the crowd." At last, Sartre exclaimed, the philosopher could be a "man among men." This article of just a few pages bristles with the excitement of a new philosophical project in the making; it would be a mistake, however, to judge that the central core of Sartre's appropriation of phenomenology was what he perceived to be its realism. As he noted in "Cartesian Freedom," a theory of autonomous thinking requires the incorporation of "productivity." He discovered this element of productivity in phenomenology's theory of constitution and it was first appropriated by Sartre in *The Transcendence of the Ego,* the work in which phenomenology is converted into an existentialist theory of freedom.

THE TRANSCENDENCE OF THE EGO

Herbert Spiegelberg in his classic, *The Phenomenological Movement,* has appropriately observed "a tendency creditable in many respects for the artist in Sartre and even for the original phenomenologist, to plunge his reader into a concrete analysis from which his real purposes emerge only gradually."[8] This is certainly the case with Sartre's most important early work, *The Transcendence of the Ego* (1935–36). He informs the reader of his thesis at the start: "We should like to show here that the ego is neither formally nor materially *in* consciousness: it is outside," and he concludes his final chapter by claiming "No more is needed in the way of a philosophical foundation for an ethics and a politics which are absolutely positive." In between he establishes the distinction between consciousness and the psychic, the freedom of consciousness, and its possibility of alienating itself. *The Transcendence of the Ego* also marks, after his initial enthusiasm, Sartre's first criticism of Husserl, for he now accuses Husserl of betraying phenomenology's fecund view of consciousness by failing to subject the ego to phenomenological reduction. In order to understand in appropriate detail how Sartre uses phenomenology to establish an existentialist view of freedom, it is necessary to first consider what he says about the structure of consciousness.

Sartre maintains the *cogito* as his philosophical point of departure. Humanist philosophy, in his estimation, must so base itself or render meaningless the radical difference between the human existent and things. Certainly, a good deal of Sartre's warmth toward Husserl was based on the consistent priority awarded by the latter to the *cogito*. Sartre's phenomenological existentialism is firmly enrooted in the *cogito* tradition, as opposed to the versions of phenomenological existentialism offered by Martin Heidegger and Maurice Merleau Ponty. Sartre, however, is careful to nuance his affiliation with the *cogito* tradition. He criticizes Descartes for seriously erring both in identifying consciousness with reflection and in making consciousness a substance.

That the Cartesian *cogito* is a reflective operation is clear. Descartes doubts, then takes his own act of doubting as the evidence required to overcome scepticism: If he doubts, then he must exist. Sartre points out that this *cogito* is "performed by a consciousness *directed upon consciousness*, a consciousness which takes consciousness as its object" (*TE,* 44). Prior to reflecting upon his doubting, Descartes was actually engaged in doubting. While actually doubting, while living the experience itself of doubting, Descartes was not thinking about his doubting. This means that Descartes's own consciousness was not, on this level, an object to itself. Sartre's point is that in any lived act one's consciousness is not an object. The prior state of the lived experience, the unreflected act, must be differentiated from the subsequent, or secondary, operation whereby a reflecting consciousness comes to bear in an objective way upon the unreflective or pre-reflective consciousness. There is then, for Sartre, a pre-reflective consciousness which is the basis for reflection. Thought becomes reintegrated into life; life, or existence, has priority over thought: "the unreflected has the ontological priority over the reflected because the unreflected consciousness does not need to be reflected in order to exist and because reflection presupposes the intervention of a second-degree consciousness" (TE, 57–58).

The other mistake Descartes made was to reify consciousness. "I am," wrote Descartes, "a real thing, and really existent; but what thing? . . . a thinking thing. . . . But what is a thinking thing? It is a thing that doubts, understands, affirms, denies, wills, refuses, that imagines also, and perceives."9 For Descartes there are things or substances that have extension in space and others, unextended, that think. By conceiving of consciousness as a thing, albeit a special thing, Descartes was victim of what Sartre calls "the illusion of immanence," and what his colleague Merleau-Ponty called "the prejudice of the world," modeling consciousness upon its objects. Objects are conceived to be units, self-contained parcels of reality, identical with themselves. Relations of these things with one another are carried on by virtue of external causality. By reifying consciousness Descartes entangled himself in that thicket of problems such as how one thing called consciousness or mind can be related to that other thing called body, or how it is possible to get things "out there" into this thing that is my consciousness. Though he meant to "save" consciousness from reduction to the mechanical world, Descartes, in making it a substance or thing and thinking of it causally, actually led the way to the psychologistic, mechanistic treatment of mind against the absurdities of which Husserl proposed phenomenology.

Husserl, in rejecting psychologism, proposed an alternative model of viewing conscious life. Consciousness is *intentional*, i.e., consciousness is a relation, act, or function rather than a thing.

> Each cogito, each consciousness process, we may also say 'means' *something or other* and bears in itself, in this manner peculiar to the *meant*, its particular *cogitatum*. . . . Conscious processes are also *intentional:* but then the word intentionality signifies nothing else than this universal fundamental property of consciousness: to be conscious *of* something as a *cogito* to bear within itself its *cogitatum*.10

We have already observed that Sartre's original enthusiasm for intentionality centered very much upon what he perceived to be its desubstantializing of consciousness: "Consciousness is purified, it is as clear as a great wind, there is nothing in it, save a movement of escape and a sliding outside itself."11 Sartre is convinced, however, that Husserl surrendered the benefits of intentionality in assuming an egological theory of intentionality. First, Sartre sees the ego as a vestige of idealism. His interpretation of Husserl's view is that behind various conscious acts resides an ego which serves as the point of identity for the multiplicity of acts. If the ego is distinct from the multiple acts, the acts stand between the ego and its objects, having the effect of making the ego appear as other-worldly. It smacks of inner-man theories that are preoccupied with cultivation of the soul. Sartre reproaches such an immanentist theory of the *ego* as being "escapist," for it has the effect of "pulling a part of man out of the world and, in that way, turning our attention from the real problems" (*TE*, 104–105). The second consequence, which will be taken up in detail shortly, is that to Sartre a pre-given ego, one that exists *prior* to and not subsequent to acts, is incompatible with freedom.

While Sartre rejects an egological theory of consciousness, he does hold that there is a self or subject. He establishes this by holding to the view that all consciousness contains self-reference as well as intentional reference to objects. On pre-reflective and reflective levels, consciousness intends objects. To characterize this intentionality Sartre often uses the terms "positional" or "thetic." The reflective consciousness intends in a positional manner the pre-reflective consciousness. Pre-reflective consciousness intends in a positional manner some object other than itself, but both levels, in addition, simultaneous with this positional intending, are non-positionally self-aware. While Descartes was doubting, he intended the objects doubted and was non-positionally aware of doing this. When he reflected upon his doubting, i.e., when he made an object of his own doubting, his reflecting consciousness was non-positionally aware of doing this. This implicit self-awareness, or sense of self, is subjectivity or self for Sartre and is a bedrock truth of his existentialism, as will be seen. All attempts to objectify this self create a realm of discourse which does not contain subjectivity. The epistemological starting point of Sartre's existential philosophy is the irreducible subject/object relationship.

> Indeed, the existence of consciousness is an absolute because consciousness is consciousness of itself. This is to say that the type of existence of consciousness is to be consciousness of itself. And consciousness is aware of itself *insofar as it is consciousness of a transcendent object*. All is therefore clear and lucid in consciousness, but consciousness is purely and simply consciousness of that object. This is the law of its existence. We should add that this consciousness of consciousness . . . is not *positional*, which is to say that consciousness is not for itself its own object. Its object is by nature outside of it. (*TE*, 40–41)

It is important to note that the implicit, or non-positional, self-awareness exists on both levels, pre-reflective and reflective. He says of the latter: "Now my reflecting consciousness does not take itself for an object when I effect the *cogito*. What it affirms concerns the reflected consciousness. Insofar as my reflecting consciousness is consciousness of itself, it is a *non-positional* consciousness" (*TE*, 44). There exists on both levels an irreducible sense of self as opposed to an objective knowledge that can be obtained about the self. *The Transcendence of the Ego* can and should be read as Sartre's indictment of objective psychology. He contends that objective psychology identifies the self as an object, reducing it to a world of analytic, causal discourse which is immune to the existential sense of self.

Sartre notes that the *I* appears upon reflection, when consciousness makes an object of itself. It is constituted through objectification and belongs to that realm of discourse, not the discourse of intentional self-awareness. By holding to an egological view of consciousness, Husserl, in Sartre's eyes, was guilty of a naiveté, taking as an original given what is really a product of the operation of consciousness. Husserl's epoché must be radicalized: "Let us be more radical and assert without fear that all *transcendence* must fall under the *epoché;* . . . the I is not of the same nature as transcendental consciousness" (*TE,* 51). Husserl depicted in *Ideas I* the difference between the "natural" and "phenomenological" attitudes, the natural attitude being one which accepts uncritically and as factually given various sorts of objects—mathematical, physical, aesthetic, etc. The natural attitude is insensitive to the beliefs, prejudices, theories that enter into the formation of these objectivities. By epoché Husserl thought it possible to put out of action the beliefs, prejudices, theories which are operative in immediate experience so that a genuine given might appear. Thus critical philosophy begins with the possibility of disengaging from the natural attitude: "Instead of remaining in this attitude, we propose to alter it radically. . . . This changing of value is a matter in which we are perfectly free. . . . We put out of action the general positing which belongs to the essence of the natural attitude; we parenthesize every thing which that positing encompasses with respect to being."[12] By effecting the epoché, the phenomenological investigator comes to see that every given is always a given-by-and-through consciousness. For every object that has a sense, there is a sense-giving intention of consciousness as its correlate. From establishing this correlation, Husserl moves to the conclusion that the world gets its entire sense, including its existential sense, from transcendental egological consciousness. "The whole *spatio-temporal world,*" he tells us, "which includes human being and the human Ego as subordinate single realities is, *according to its sense, a merely intentional being,* thus one has the merely secondary sense of a being for a consciousness."[13] While Husserl relegates the "human ego" to a secondary, relative status, he claims that transcendental consciousness is irreducibly egological, failing to see, in Sartre's judgment, that the Transcendental Ego is a product. The Sartrean structure of consciousness presents the first level of consciousness (unreflected consciousness), the realm of lived experience, as Ego-less. "The consciousness which says I think is precisely not the consciousness which thinks." It is the reflective consciousness, the consciousness directed upon thinking, which says "I think." The thinking consciousness is limited to intending (thinking) objects and being non-positionally aware of itself in the process. Sartre tells us that "When I run after a streetcar . . . there is no *I*. There is consciousness *of-the-streetcar-having-to-be-overtaken* . . . and nonpositional consciousness of consciousness" (*TE,* 48–49).

Making the Ego a structure of transcendental consciousness is un-phenomenological, according to Sartre. First of all the Ego is not transcendental since "it affirms its permanence beyond this consciousness and all consciousness," that is, it is transcendent with respect to an intuitive grasp of consciousness. Second, it is not even required as a postulate to account for the unity of transcendental experience, for as Husserl himself had stated in his lectures on internal time, consciousness unifies itself through a sort of snowballing effect, "a play of 'transversal' intentionalities," whereby the present retains the past and projects the future without having to objectively represent either. Sartre does not pause to develop his own theory of the continuity of experience here. In *Being and Nothingness,* he will attempt to account for the continuity of a self in terms both of temporality and of what he will call original project.

Having distinguished the psychic (objective) from the transcendental consciousness, Sartre goes on to show how the psychic is constituted through reflection. The Ego shows two psychic faces: the *I*, which is the Ego as the unity of actions, and the *me*, which is the unity of states and of qualities. Failure to distinguish the transcendental from the psychic constitutes an "impure" reflection resulting in a psychology that reifies consciousness, rendering it inert, mechanical, and passive. Lived experiences are objectified into states and affixed to the Ego as their source. This impure reflection actually reverses the order of constitution: "But as the order is reversed by a consciousness which imprisons itself in the world in order to flee from itself, consciousnesses are given as emanating from states, and states as produced by the ego" (*TE,* 81). An impure reflection confuses objectified consciousness with actual, existential consciousness. Notice that Sartre does not consider this confusion to be a mere mistake or an innocent naiveté, but a "flight from itself." His criticism of Descartes and Husserl has sharply turned toward significant "existential" and moral considerations. Transcendental consciousness is not a product of the Ego. It is, rather, an *impersonal spontaneity* which is not the product of anything but itself: "nothing can act on consciousness because it is cause of itself. . . . Each instant of our conscious life reveals to us a creation *ex nihilo*" (*TE,* 82, 98–99). Causality is a valid way of thinking about the relation of objects or things to one another. It would be a serious category mistake, however, to apply a mode of object relations to transcendental consciousness, which is not an object. Transcendental consciousness, we must recall, is act, is an intentional presentation of objects, without itself being reduced to the status of an object. The eviction of the Ego from transcendental consciousness throws us headlong into Sartre's radical conception of freedom. He uses an example to display this freedom: "A young bride was in terror, when her husband left her alone, of sitting at the window and summoning the passers-by like a prostitute" (*TE,* 100). The young woman evidently believed herself to be something, a certain kind of person ("I am married," "I am faithful," etc.) and was terrified because her "consciousness suddenly appeared to itself as infinitely overflowing in its possibilities, the *I* which ordinarily serves as its unity" (*TE*, 100). She had thought that her possible actions (and correlatively the "world" which offered itself to be "acted upon" were limited, and discovered, to the contrary, that she was "monstrously free." Nothing could prevent her from acting as a prostitute. She then became obsessed with the idea. The meaning of her anxiety was that she comprehended her true transcendental freedom, which contested the objectified representation of herself, her Ego. Sartre's remarks scattered throughout *The Transcendence of the Ego* to the effect that making the Ego a structure of transcendental consciousness would "load down" the latter and make it "heavy and ponderable" now become clear. In his judgment, if the Ego were in consciousness our conscious acts would not be free; they would flow from a source, deriving as it were from a nature, which would incline our actions in certain directions. The young woman in question would be capable only of the actions of a "married" and "faithful" nature. If, on the contrary, consciousness springs from itself, then it is radically free to choose its activity, its "identity."

The theme of responsibility is correlative with that of freedom and understandably appears in *The Transcendence of the Ego*. As Husserl had depicted the natural attitude, it involved a *loss* of subjectivity, in the sense that consciousness, in lived experience, did not notice itself as constituting its objects. The phenomenological reduction *restored* subjectivity to its constitutive function vis-à-vis the world. If, as Sartre has argued, the Ego is transcendent to consciousness, the belief that consciousness is identical to the Ego is itself a natural attitude belief. In terms of Sartre's position, this means that the natural attitude involves in some sense a *loss* of freedom.

This loss of freedom, or *self-alienation*, which is its true name, is not ontological. Transcendental consciousness, in its being, remains thoroughly free, so that *it must put itself into a state* (natural attitude) in which it diminishes itself, or better, hides itself. Given the structure of consciousness as pure act and perpetual self-creation, it is impossible to accept that this alienation is inflicted on consciousness, caused in it from the outside. Consciousness must inflict this alienation upon itself. (Recall Sartre's remark, referred to earlier, about a consciousness which "imprisons itself in the world in order to flee from itself.") "Everything happens, therefore, as if consciousness constituted the ego as a false representation of itself, as if consciousness hypnotized itself before this ego as if to make the ego its guardian and its law. Consciousness is frightened by its own spontaneity. . . . Perhaps the essential role of the ego is to mask from consciousness its very spontaneity" (*TE* 101, 100).

It is possible for consciousness, through the epoché, to move itself from its alienation. Consciousness can "suddenly" produce itself "on the pure reflective level" where it sees itself "maintaining the ego outside itself by a continuous creation" (*TE*, 101). The "pure reflective level" is equated with effecting a phenomenological reduction. For Sartre, effecting the epoché is equivalent to a veritable *conversion* (in *Being and Nothingness* he will refer to it as a "radical conversion") of one's life. This is what he means toward the end of *The Transcendence of the Ego* when he tells us that "the 'εποχή is not simply an intellectual method; an erudite procedure: it is an anxiety which is imposed on us and which we cannot avoid" (*TE,* 103). The epoché, experienced as anguish, is the grasp of consciousness by itself as excluding any pre-given contents, such as an Ego, which would restrict its activities. For Sartre, the epoché forms the basis of a presuppositionless ethic which casts total responsibility for all actions upon the individual consciousness. It must be emphasized that Sartre clearly thinks that the attitude of impure reflection or flight can be overcome by an attitude of assuming respon-sibility for one's life. This is a matter that we will have occasion to treat in detail later, when we consider the alleged pessimism of *Being and Nothingness.*

These last mentioned texts deserve attention, for they bear directly on the issue of Sartre's appropriation of phenomenology. The concluding line of *The Transcendence of the Ego,* in which Sartre sees the thrust of the book's argument to be "a philosophical foundation for an ethics and a politics" (*TE,* 106), provides the context for understanding that appropriation. In the texts we just referred to, Sartre distinguishes two opposed attitudes— the attitude of impure reflection or flight, whereby consciousness attempts to identify itself with its constituted product (the Ego), and the attitude of pure reflection, whereby consciousness grasps itself as the constitutive source of the Ego. These attitudes roughly correspond to Husserl's natural and phenomenological attitudes, although the irony of *The Transcendence of the Ego* is that Husserl is accused of naively retaining the Ego within transcendental consciousness. It is thus misleading to assert, as so many commentators do, that the phenomenological reduction plays no role in Sartre's thought. Indeed, the fact is that he employs the reduction as the entry into assuming an authentic existence.[14] His appropriation of the reduction discloses the productive capacity of consciousness to constitute various forms of givenness. We will see shortly that he refuses to reduce all forms of givenness, but it would be incorrect to judge that Sartre's phe-nomenology limited itself to simply describing, in realistic fashion, various forms of givenness. He is constantly searching out forms of givenness comprised of congealed meanings that, while being constituted products of consciousness, are used by consciousness as a means of disguising its free-dom.

THE PROJECT

The power of consciousness is displayed in *The Transcendence of the Ego* in the notion of self-creative spontaneity and purifying reflection. Both of these notions will appear in *Being and Nothingness* and will be discussed in the following chapter. For the present, we will examine what Sartre refers to as "project" in *Being and Nothingness* as a further application of the theory of reduced freedom proposed in *The Transcendence of the Ego*.

In the first chapter of *Being and Nothingness*, Sartre uses the example of an alarm clock in the course of presenting existential freedom.

> The alarm which rings in the morning refers to the possibility of my going to work, which is *my* possibility. But to apprehend the summons of the alarm as a summons is to get up. Therefore, the very act of getting up is reassuring, for it eludes the question, 'Is work my possibility?' Consequently it does not put me in a position to apprehend the possibility of questions of refusing to work, and finally the possibility of refusing the world and the possibility of death. In short, to the extent that I apprehend the meaning of the ringing, I am already up at its summons, this apprehension guarantees me against the anguished intuition that it is I who confer on the alarm clock its exigency—I and I alone. (*BN*, 77–78)

The sound of the alarm is perceived as a meaningful sound, as an exigency over me. The meaning/exigency derives from my projects of work, of sustaining life, of spending salary to buy pen and paper to be a writer. A suspension (epoché) and stepping back from the immediate situation generates a reductive analysis to what Sartre will call "one's original project" later on in *Being and Nothingness*. A project is an activity undertaken to realize an end, and projective activity is what characterizes human beings. An epoché of one's life would thematize a number of on-going projects, some enveloping others, but one overriding project that forms the context for the meaning of all the others. If one's original project is to be a writer, it forms the intelligibility (not in cause/effect discourse) of the other projects—of wanting to live, associating with certain people, adopting a lifestyle of a particular sort, etc. The noise of the alarm is not a mere physical stimulus impinging upon a passive organism. Human beings live in a *world*, not of stimuli but of "instrumental complexes," of various meanings and values, and the "world" in that sense of the term is constituted by the original project. What confronts the self receives a sense, value, interpretation in terms of the interests of the self. The original project defines what will serve as "stimuli" for it by providing the context of significance.

While an individual's life expresses in various ways the original choice, the original choice, Sartre claims, is *unjustifiable:* "This means that we apprehend our choice as not deriving from any prior reality but rather as being about to serve as foundation for the ensemble of significations which constitute reality" (*BN*, 464). The world of meaning and value has a foundation in choice, but choice itself has no foundation, or, Sartre reasons, it would not be choice. Choice can only be conceived as pure spontaneity, pure act: "Indeed it is impossible for a determined process to act upon a spontaneity, exactly as it is impossible for objects to act upon consciousness" (*BN*, 442). Spontaneity is totally separated from passivity: "For human reality, to be is to choose *oneself;* nothing comes to it from the outside or from within which it can *receive* or *accept*" (*BN*, 440). Because an individual's original project defines all his or her other, less inclusive projects, and this original choice is itself unjustifiable, the individual lives with the potential to change the original project by "an abrupt metamorphosis of my initial project—i.e., by another choice of myself and of my ends. Moreover, this modification is always possible" (*BN*, 464). The individual is always "haunted by the specter of the instant" (*BN*, 467), of a break in one project and assumption of another. Human existence is constantly "troubled."

By identifying freedom and the structure of consciousness, Sartre commits himself to the view that every act of consciousness is a free spontaneity: "man can not be sometimes slave and sometimes free; he is wholly and forever free or he is not free at all" (*BN*, 461). Thus even in affectivity, in emotional life, where it appears that consciousness is in the grasp of overwhelming passion. Sartre insists that conscousness makes itself emotional. He goes so far as to hold that mental illness also is a choice, "an invention so as to be able to live an unlivable situation."[15] The early works propose an existential psychology as replacement for the prevalent behavioral, mechanistic psychologies. The stimulus-organism-response model of the latter stresses the organism's passivity and lack of finality, while Sartre offers a view centered upon intentionality conceived of as active, self-conscious, spontaneous. Intentionally acting human beings live in a world of meaning and value grounded not in being but in the very activity of the intentional self. All human behavior is active and intentional. It is true that Sartre often focuses upon imagination in portraying the freedom of consciousness to disengage from the world. While emphasis is usually put on imaginative consciousness, both by Sartre and by his commentators, even perception displays that power of conscousness. In perception, the perceiver attends to objects as foreground, selecting them from the horizon by virtue of his or her interest. "We must observe that in perception there is always the construction of a figure on a ground. No one object, no group of objects is especially designed to be organized as specifically either ground or figure; we depend on the distinction of my attention" (*BN*, 9). The project defines that interest. Even perceptual consciousness is, by Sartre's definition, present to itself, thereby at a distance from its objects and beyond their control. The power of consciousness is located in its structure, which precludes the identity of consciousness with its object or with itself.

We have argued that Sartre found through his reading of Husserl the technical philosophy that could organize and inform his desire to make philosophy out of concrete experience and to develop a humanistic ethic. Within the technicalities of Husserl's phenomenology, Sartre was especially attracted by the notions of "intentionality" and "reduction," the creative and constitutive functions of consciousness. In his novel *Nausea* (1938) he recognized the *facticity* of the free self, that it found itself existing in a situation that was not of the self's choosing. Nonetheless, in the writings up to and including *Being and Nothingness*, a probing of the situation was not his main concern. While he recognized that the free self through its projects constituted a world of meaning and value, the way that he presented freedom smacked of stoicism and quietism. His interest was in preserving the freedom of the self from determination by the world or by Others. He argued that the self was responsible for its situation, but offered no program for changing the situation. His own analysis of this existential stoicism in his autobiography, *The Words*, will lay blame on his socialization, and not on the phenomenological method which supported his early philosophy.

It should not be surprising that Sartre, at the conclusion of *The Transcendence of the Ego* and *Being and Nothingness*, should see ethical and political implications in the phenomenological tools of intentionality, reduction, and constitution, for Husserl had firmly grasped this himself. In fact, Husserl saw this as the very meaning of his phenomenological project. It may appear odd to propose that Husserl and Sartre shared similar philosophical programs. In his article "The Phenomenological Philosophy in France,"[16] Ian Alexander likens the impact of Husserl on French thought to that of Wittgenstein on British thought: "The result in both cases has been to revolutionize the philosophical perspective." When he goes on to assess individual philosophers, his judgment is that "of French phenomenologists [Gabriel] Marcel and Merleau-Ponty come closest to its essential aim." This judgment is commonplace, that the fruition of phenomenology is an existential philosophy deriving from Husserl's treatment, in his later work, of the grounding of consciousness in the pre-theoretical life-world. Merleau-Ponty and Marcel in France and Heidegger in Germany developed phenomenologies of being-in-the-world stressing finitude, which featured the imbeddedness of consciousness in its situation. Sartre's phenomenology of subjectivity stresses autonomy, and features the transcendence of consciousness over its situation. A strong case can be made that, in doing this, it was Sartre (unwittingly perhaps) and not the others who was the more faithful to Husserl's program. While at first sight the philosopher of the cafés and the German academician appear to inhabit two vastly different philosophical worlds, it is possible to find a common ground between them. To do this, it is necessary to turn to those texts where Husserl talks about the task of philosophy and, in particular, of his own philosophical "mission."

In a letter to Arnold Metzger, dated September 1919,[17] Husserl replies to Metzger who has sent his work to Husserl for comment. He tells Metzger: "It can only be that you felt, through the unadorned soberness and radical objectivity of my writings, the personal ethos on which they rest."[18] Throughout this interesting letter, Husserl uses the expressions "my mission," "my true, god-sent mission," "the deeper meaning of my work," and "my original motives and needs." The writings Metzger sent Husserl dwelt on the themes of freedom, death, and value. While Husserl told Metzger that the latter's "ethical radicalism . . . rejoiced my heart," nonetheless he expressed disappointment that transcendental phenomenology was not used by Metzger as the foundation for his very practical concerns. Husserl applauds Metzger for seeing that "every form of anthropologism, biologism, positivism turns into an anti-ethical, ethically groundless . . . egoism,"[19] but criticizes Metzger's failure to see transcendental phenomenology's relevance to "the practical design of ends." In fact, Husserl goes as far as saying that truth and scientific knowledge do not count for him as the highest value. His entire project to found a scientific philosophy flows from his "deepest impulses," from an "inexpressible need of the soul," which seems to have been precipitated from a reading of the New Testament leading "to an impulse to find the way to God and a true life through a strictly scientific philosophy."[20]

Some years previously, Husserl had published an outline of his philosophical projects under the title "Philosophy as a Rigorous Science" (1910–11). His opening sentences connect the project of rigorous science to that of ethics: "From its earliest beginnings philosophy has claimed to be rigorous science. What is more, it has claimed to be the science that satisfies the loftiest theoretical needs and renders possible from an ethico-religious point of view a life regulated by pure rational norms."[21] He sees philosophy as a "vocation" whose task it is "to teach us how to carry on the eternal work of humanity."[22] Since he embraces this lofty idea of philosophy, Husserl sees that philosophy must bear on culture. Setting the context of his work, he tells us that he writes out of "the conviction that the highest interests of human culture demand the development of a rigorously scientific philosophy."[23] Consequently he accepts the burden of responsibility for humanity: "we remain aware of the responsibility we have in regard to humanity."[24] When he attacks naturalism, psychologism, and historicism, he does so because he sees them as "a growing danger to our culture," for these objectivistic views of consciousness lead to sceptical absurdity or relativism in the realm of values. A "remedy" is called for in the form of a critique of reason, a transcendental phenomenology, which will lay the foundation for a true ethic:

> If depressing absurdities in the interpretation of the world are connected with such prejudices, then there is only one remedy for these and all similar evils: a scientific critique and in addition a radical science, issuing from below, based on sure foundations, and progressing according to the most rigorous methods—the philosophical science for which we speak here.[25]

Toward the end of his life, in the "Prague" and "Vienna" lectures included in *The Crisis of European Sciences and Transcendental Phenomenology* (1938), when Husserl was presenting his phenomenology on a new footing, he again refers to the ethical context of his work. He condemns science for a positivistic attitude toward "the questions which are decisive for a genuine humanity," questions which "concern man as a free, self-determining being in his behavior toward the human and extra-human surrounding world and free in regard to his capacities for rationally shaping himself and his surrounding world."[26] It would be a mistake to consider this attitude as the superficial adoption of an existentialist (particularly Heideggerian) viewpoint that was then in vogue—a window dressing, as it were, for Husserl's epistemology and idealism. Such an interpretation would overlook the ideas clearly expressed in the Metzger letter and in "Philosophy as a Rigorous Science." The language of "self-determination" (Husserl, like Sartre, often refers to the "autonomy" of consciousness) is crucial for putting into perspective the much-discussed theme of the "life-world" in the *Crisis*. Contrary to those commentators (and it appears that Ian Alexander is one of these) who see in the life-world theme a radical break from Husserl's former program, it is clear that Husserl continues to emphasize the capacity of consciousness to disengage from the life-world, to effect an epoché of culture so that the life-world can be critiqued. Husserl in no way thinks that we are so embedded in the life-world that its norms and values can not or ought not to be questioned. On the contrary, he insists that "the whole *praxis* of human existence, i.e., the whole of cultural life, must receive its norms not from the naive experience and tradition of everyday life but from objective truth."[27] The life-world, subjected to the epoché, is brought within the scope of human constitution: "every fact given under the heading of 'culture,' whether it is a matter of the lowliest culture of necessities or the highest culture (science, state, church, economic organization, etc.), is something constructed through human activity."[28]

The key to the transformation between living "naively" (alienated) and assuming rational responsibility for one's self and one's culture is the effecting of the reduction. We have adverted to the fact that, for Sartre, the existential impact of performing the reduction was equivalent to a "conversion" of one's life. This was also true for Husserl, as a passage from his *Crisis* makes clear:

> There are good reasons for my stressing so sharply the vocational character of even the phenomenologist's attitude. Perhaps it will even become manifest that the total phenomenological attitude and the epoché belonging to it are destined in essence to effect, at first, a complete personal transformation, comparable in the beginning to a religious conversion, which then, however, over and above this, bears within itself the significance of the greatest existential transformation which is assigned as a task to mankind as such.[29]

Sartre did not have a scholar's knowledge of Husserl's works. His genius was to see, primarily through a reading of *Ideas I*, the ethical implication of basic phenomenological concepts. What Sartre grasped in Husserl's project was a paradigm of critique and autonomous control centered upon the power of consciousness. Sartre took up that paradigm to give expression to his own intuitions of freedom and contingency, but within the scope of that paradigm both thinkers issued a call to men responsibly to shape their selves and their culture.

By stressing the eidetic structure as the same in all intentional acts, and grounding freedom and active sense of self in this structure, Sartre is led to claim that the self is wholly free and wholly present to itself in all of its acts. Whether on the pre-reflective or the reflective level, consciousness is free and its choices unjustifiable. In fact, even when one reflectively deliberates, "the chips are already down," since any criterion or motive for electing one alternative over another must itself be unjustifiably chosen. If deliberation implies criteria, the criteria play their role in a decisive but assumed manner. It is unclear from Sartre's existential theory of freedom as presented thus far why he prizes pure reflection, since one would not be any freer through it. He does refer in *The Transcendence of the Ego* to the natural attitude as "flight" and "escape," and in the example of the alarm clock he speaks of an avoidance of questioning which "guarantees me against the anguished intuition" that I am the foundation of my life. In *Being and Nothingness* he will concentrate on flight behavior, offering an analysis of its types and motives, as well as pointing out the possibility and value of overcoming it. And since his theory of the active, free self heavily stresses the constitution of a world of meaning and value, he will offer an ontology that will guarantee the reality of forms of otherness-than-self.

Self/Other

While *Being and Nothingness* can be considered to be a synthesis of the major concerns of the earlier works—freedom, contingency, flight—its aims are limited. Sartre has referred to *Being and Nothingness*, retrospectively, as his "eidetic of bad faith"[1] and "an ontology before conversion" (*C*, 13). Specifically, *Being and Nothingness* lays out certain invariant structures (modalities of being) of the life-world, shows how these structures enable and motivate bad faith, presents a portrait of the attitude of bad faith, and points the way, through a theory of reflection, toward the overcoming of bad faith. In the process, the themes of freedom, contingency, and flight receive a new level of intelligibility.

In advertising his theory of being as "phenomenological ontology," Sartre claims not only a thematic but also a methodological tie with his early work. It can be expected that the theory of being will be joined to the theory of experience and reflection he had previously developed. As we have observed, however, the early work revealed a heavy, even one-sided, emphasis upon the capacity of consciousness to impose meaning to the detriment of due attentiveness to the implantation of consciousness in the world.[2] We will look at the conjunction in *Being and Nothingness* of the theory of being and the theory of reflection to determine whether, on the ontological level, Sartre can clarify the relation of the transcending power of consciousness to its situatedness in the world.

ONTOLOGICAL PROOF

The heart of the controversial introduction to *Being and Nothingness* is the "ontological proof," which purports "to distinguish two absolutely separated regions of being" (*BN*, lxiii): being-for-itself and being-in-itself. These two modalities of being, along with being-for-Others, which is taken up in part three of *Being and Nothingness*, comprise for Sartre the basic ontological structures of phenomenological ontology. The brevity and ambiguity with which the proof is presented have led to sharp debates about its meaning and validity, and, since this proof appears essential to the remainder of *Being and Nothingness*, problems with the proof have translated into problems with the entire project.

The proof consists in a statement of the principle of intentionality, followed immediately by a claim regarding the grounds of its possibility: "Consciousness is consciousness *of* something. This means that transcendence is the constitutive structure of consciousness: that is, that consciousness is born *supported* by a being which is not itself" (*BN*, lxi). In the brief comments that follow, Sartre clarifies that he is not proposing an epistemological argument that a subject requires an object, but rather an ontological statement concerning the being of the subject: "this being implies a being other than itself" (*BN*, lxii). There is scant basis, in the introduction, for understanding the proof. Only deep into the text, in the chapters on "Temporality" and "Transcendence," does he return to articulating the proof again, this time in the context of his theory of negation and difference. In the chapter on "Temporality," he writes:

> Furthermore in itself the For-itself is not being, for it makes itself be explicitly for-itself as not being being. It is consciousness of——as the internal negation of——. The structure at the basis of intentionality and of selfness is the negation, which is the *internal* relation of the for-itself to the thing. (*BN*, 123)

In the following chapter, "Transcendence," he returns again to his ontological interpretation of intentionality.

> It is the very being of the for-itself in so far as this is presence to——; that is, in so far as the for-itself has to be its being by making itself not to be a certain being to which it is present. This means that the for-itself can be only in the mode of a reflection [*reflet*] causing itself to be reflected as not being a certain being. . . . The reflected causes itself to be qualified *outside* next to a certain being as *not being* that being. This is precisely what we mean by "to be consciousness *of* something." (*BN*, 174)

The ontological proof thus hinges on the theory of negation. The entire discussion of the "separate regions of being," however, finds its roots in Sartre's reading of Husserl and in his on-going quarrel with him.

We have observed in *The Transcendence of the Ego* how Sartre tempered his early enthusiasm for Husserl, so apparent in the brief article on intentionality. In *Being and Nothingness*, Sartre has made up his mind about Husserl: he is an idealist who both betrays and misunderstands the principle of intentionality: "he is totally unfaithful to his principle"; "he misunderstood its essential character" (*BN*, lxi). Specifically, he alleges that Husserl made of the noema an "unreal . . . a noema whose *esse* is percipi" (*BN*, lxi), thereby forfeiting the realism that attracted Sartre to phenomenology.

In the early article on intentionality Sartre assumed that he and Husserl agreed on the intentional nature of consciousness. Things are not *in* but *relative* to consciousness: "this tree on its bit of parched earth is not an absolute which would subsequently enter into communication with us, consciousness and world are given at one stroke: essentially external to consciousness, the world is essentially relative to consciousness."³ Consciousness and world are presented as having different "natures." The tree "could not enter into your consciousness, for it is not of the same nature as consciousness." Indeed, in *Ideas I*, Sartre found Husserl also preserving the sharp distinction between consciousness and its objects. In the second chapter, "Consciousness and Natural Actuality," Husserl engages in a "psychological phenomenological" inquiry into the essence of experience in its dimensions of *cogitatio* and *cogitatum*. He points out that immanent objects of consciousness (conscious acts reflected upon) are to be distinguished from objects transcendent to consciousness, such as a perceived sheet of paper: "this sheet of paper given on the mental process of perception, is by essential necessity not a mental process but a *being of a wholly different mode of being*"⁴ (emphasis added). Husserl further clarifies that this radical difference in modality of being between consciousness and object holds beyond perception, in the case of recollection, for example, and fancies:

> Of these essentially different mental processes obviously everything is true that we adduced about mental processes of perception. We shall not think of confusing the *objects intended to in* these modes of consciousness (for example, the phantasied water nymphs) with the mental processes themselves of consciousness which are consciousness *of* these objects.⁵

The *cogitata* of various intentional experiences are characterized as "transcendent," "other," "something alien," with respect to their corresponding *cogitationes*. Given this essential difference Husserl raises several questions about their relationship:

> To what extent, in the first place, is the *material world* something of an essentially different kind excluded from the *essentiality proper of mental processes?* And if that is true of the material world, if the material world stands in contrast to all consciousness, [and to the own-essentiality of consciousness,] as '*something alien*,' the '*otherness*,' then how *can* consciousness become involved with it—with the material world and consequently with the *whole* world other than consciousness?⁶

In particular, if perceiving consciousness and the material world belonged to the same fundamental stratum and formed a real unity, then there could be no difference in nature between them, which would lead to causal theories of mind and their psychologistic consequences. Monism would appear to preclude the subject/object differentiation required of true cognition: "How does, and how can, *consciousness itself* become separated out as a *concrete being in* itself? And how does that which is intended to in it, the *perceived being*, become separated out as 'over against' consciousness and as '*in itself and by itself*'?"⁷ Husserl poses a dilemma for traditional epistemologies. If consciousness and its transcendent objects are so "heterogeneous" and "alien," how can they become involved? And if they share a community of essence to explain their involvement, then how can their essential differences be preserved? The dilemma is posed as rationale for effecting the phenomenological reduction in the following chapter. Sartre in fact opposes the reduction insofar as it ultimately neutralizes the epistemological difference between subject and object, which is on the ontological level the difference between self and Other. In this context must be understood his allegation against Husserl on the issue of intentionality, which "is his essential discovery. But from the moment that he makes of the *noema* an *unreal*, a correlate *of* the *noesis* a noema whose *esse* is *percipi*, he is totally unfaithful to his principles" (*BN*, lxi). In *Being and Nothingness*, and specifically in the ontological proof, Sartre can be viewed as attempting to retrieve phenomenology from what he perceives to be Husserl's idealism. By adopting a theory of negation Sartre hopes to resolve Husserl's dilemma concerning the relationship of heterogeneity between consciousness and object.

In *The Transcendence of the Ego*, Sartre had declared his methodological commitment to the subject/object model.

> Consciousness is aware of itself *insofar as it is consciousness of a transcendent object*. All is therefore clear and lucid in consciousness: the object with its characteristic opacity is before consciousness, but consciousness is purely and simply consciousness of being consciousness of that object. This is the law of its existence. (*TE*, 40)

While rejecting the primacy of the reflective Cartesian *cogito*, Sartre embraced a primacy of a pre-reflective consciousness that possessed a remarkable likeness to the former. Pre-reflective consciousness is by no means a pure immediacy (something perhaps attributable to animals). Reflexivity appears already in the pre-reflective consciousness insofar as consciousness on this primary level is not exhausted in its positing of objects. Pre-reflective consciousness is non-positionally aware of itself; as Sartre put it in *Being and Nothingness*, it is "present to self." Sartre, in fact, was often inconsistent in his presentation of pre-reflective consciousness. For example, as we have observed, in *The Transcendence of the Ego* he depicts it as "purely and simply consciousness of being consciousness of that object." Yet, also in *The Transcendence of the Ego*, he claims that by non-positional self-consciousness, "consciousness *knows* itself only as absolute inwardness" (emphasis added; *TE*, 41). The inconsistency is carried into *Being and Nothingness* and infects, as we shall see, several important issues. What is at stake is the question of the *self* and its comprehension of itself on the pre-reflective level. It would appear that self-consciousness is at the heart of the ontological and epistemological distinctions of self/other and subject/object, respectively. There could be no awareness of what is other than self were there no contrasting apprehension of self, nor any awareness of an object as distinct from subject were there no self-apprehension on the part of the subject. In fact Sartre conflates the notions of self and subject. "What can properly be called subjectivity is consciousness (of) consciousness" (*BN*, lxi). This very relation constitutes the self: "the self is an indication of the subject himself. The *self* therefore represents an ideal distance within the immanence of the subject in relation to himself" (*BN*, 77). Thus, the ontological proof is given with Sartre's definition of the self. The self is the relation of non-positional self-consciousness, which relation in turn depends upon a positing of an object other than itself. The ontological proof concerns the disclosure of being. The coming to appearance of being requires a fundamental negation or difference, both ontologically (self/other) and epistemologically (subject/object). Thus, "the for-itself can be only in the mode of a reflection [*reflet*] causing itself to be reflected as not being a certain being. . . . This is precisely what we mean by 'to be consciousness *of* something' " (*BN*, 174).

FOR-ITSELF AND IN-ITSELF

The being of the self, as present to itself (non-positionally), while being present to an object other than itself, implies a double negation under the principle that "*presence to* always implies duality, at least a virtual separation" (*BN*, 173). There is first the negation/difference between the self and its transcendent objects: "what is present to me is not me" (*BN*, 173). Then there is the negation of the presence of consciousness to itself non-positionally: "If being is present to itself, it is because it is not wholly itself" (*BN*, 77). This latter negation is constitutive of the being of the self, which is "to exist as a being which perpetually effects in itself a break in being" (*BN*, 78). The perpetual break in being is nothing other than the temporality of the self. To exist temporally is to be wrenched from identity, from a repose in oneself: "Anything which can be present to——cannot be at rest 'in-itself' " (*BN*, 176). The for-itself refracts into past, present, and future. Sartre ontologizes these distinctions as disruptions by negation, breakages of identity. At their center in place of prominence is the present, which is "presence to . . . ," effecting the break in being and carrying it on as continual "flight from" being. The past is surpassed by the present. While my past is *my* past, I am it in the mode of "was," secreting a distinction, and thus negation, between it and the present. The ontological discourse of negation serves to preserve a certain autonomy for the present moment, founding Sartre's contention in *The Transcendence of the Ego* that each present moment is a creation *ex nihilo:* "that heavy plenitude of being (the past) is behind me, there is an absolute distance which cuts it from me and makes it fall out of my reach, without contact, without connections" (*BN*, 118).

The focus of *Being and Nothingness* is upon the being of the self, being for-itself. As a "break in being" the for-itself is shown to be temporal and radically free, responsible for its actions and attitudes. While, on the whole, critics and commentators generally agree on what Sartre means by the modality of being for-itself, there is a noticeable lack of precision on their part over what Sartre means by the modality of being in-itself. "Things," "matter," matter's "resistance," "natural thing," "all that is not human," and "unconscious being" have been offered as characterizations of being-in-itself. I am convinced that the very notion of the in-itself is a muddled one because Sartre fluctuates, in presenting the notion, between a phenomenological ontology and a speculative metaphysics.

From the perspective of phenomenology the notion of for-itself and in-itself are reciprocally intelligible. We have observed how Sartre opposed the temporal self to a being "at rest 'in itself.'" Aron Gurwitsch, in his fine study "On the Intentionality of Consciousness," points out the reciprocal intelligibility of the notions of temporality and identity in Husserl's analysis of the intentional life of consciousness. For Husserl, conscious experience is a "stream," and the multiple, changing noeses are distinguished from the self-same noema as reciprocally opposed notions. According to Gurwitsch "we may not render identity of noema explicit and ascertain it by an original experience unless we become aware of the temporality of consciousness."[8] Throughout *Being and Nothingness* the most persistent characterization of being-in-itself is that of *identity*. Being-in-itself is a region of being ruled by the principle of identity: "Is this not precisely the definition of the in-itself—or if you prefer—the principle of identity?" (*BN*, 58). But this characteristic is revealed in opposition to the temporal self-surpassing of the for-itself: "the waiter in the café cannot be immediately a café waiter in the sense that this inkwell *is* an inkwell, or the glass is a glass" (*BN*, 59). The being of individual phenomena (objects) is characterized as identity, self-sameness, and this characterization depends upon its contrast with the ever-on-going, never-self-identical being of the for-itself, which is "pure spontaneity" (*BN*, lix).

It is true that material perceptible objects are commonly given as examples of individual, self-identical objects in *Being and Nothingness:* tables, rocks, lamps, a package of tobacco. It is incontestable however that Sartre employs the principle of identity and the designation "in-itself" to quite an array of phenomena. The past is in-itself: "a for-itself fixed in in-itself" (*BN*, 202); "the Ego is in-itself, not for-itself" (*BN*, 103); "the psychic is nothing other than the in-itself" (*BN*, 162); "the odor which I suddenly breathe in with my eyes closed, even before I have referred it to an odorous object, is already an odor being . . . a being which is what it is" (*BN*, 187–88); "probabilities, which are the meaning of being beyond being, are *in-itself*" (*BN*, 197); "an established lack or a lack *in-itself*" (*BN*, 198); the body of another which appears to me and I who appear to the Look of the Other are fixed in the in-itself.

Perhaps the most interesting example of the correlation between the in-itself and the modality of objectification is the last example, that of the objectification of a consciousness. To look at another human being is to constitute him or her as an object. The Other-as-object is a "privileged object" since he or she is observed to seek ends, to have projects. However, insofar as I observe the Other in the course of working out projects, "the Other is still an object for me" and there is no need to forge another ontological modality different from for-itself and in-itself. The Other's possibilities are, as objective phenomena, "transcended," "established," "fixed," "solidified," and have the "character of the in-itself" (BN, 266).

> There, for example, is a man who is reading while he walks. The disintegration of the universe which he represents is purely virtual; he has ears which do not hear, eyes which see nothing except his book. Between his book and him I apprehend an undeniable relation without distance of the same type as that which earlier connected the walker with the grass. But this time the form has closed in on itself. There is a full object for me to grasp. In the midst of the world I can say 'man-reading' as I could say 'cold stone,' 'fine rain." I apprehend a closed 'Gestalt' in which the reading forms the essential quality; for the rest, it remains blind and mute, lets itself be known and perceived as a pure and simple temporal-spatial thing, and seems to be related to the rest of the world by a purely indifferent externality. (BN, 256)

If I am looked at by the Other, I experience a new modality of my being, objectification, through which I become—for the Other—in-itself. "Shame reveals to me that I *am* this being, not in the mode of 'was' or of 'having to be' but in-itself" (BN, 262). What these various phenomena referred to as the in-itself share as a core meaning is identity, reified presence, externality to the self, givenness—in short, a mode of objectified being whose sense is constituted in contrast with the temporal self-surpassing of the for-itself. The in-itself is not a particular object, but the modality of object-being: "a mode of being . . . radically different from the mode of being 'for-itself'" (BN, 188). This can be clearly grasped in his discussion of the mode of being of a "quality," which is not a physical thing. He uses the example of "light which strikes my eyes in the morning through my closed lids" (BN, 188), designating it as a "light-being." A quality, he insists, *is* "as a being which is what it is" and, possessing this identity, is irreducible to subjectivity—"it cannot be inserted in the woof of that subjectivity which is what it is not and which is not what it is." Thus a quality is "radically" different from the mode of being-for-itself. A quality is not a "thing" but is an appearance, i.e., an object which is what it is. An object or appearance appears with an identity and therefore is different in being from the spontaneity of the for-itself "which is what it is not and which is not what it is." A few lines after this passage, Sartre states that something is "in-itself in that it does not in any way belong to the for-itself" (BN, 190). Because the for-itself is "break in being," temporal self-surpassing, no transcendent object belongs to the being of the for-itself. An object appears as reified, given, the same, in opposition to the being of the conscious self. In *The Transcendence of the Ego*, in formulating his understanding of intentionality, Sartre said of consciousness that "its object is by nature outside of it" (*TE*, 41) and that "the object is transcendent to the consciousness which grasps it" (*TE*, 38). In *Being and Nothingness* we are to understand that consciousness and object do not have a common essence or mode of being but rather heterogeneous modes of being: "the for-itself puts its own being in question as not being the being of the object" (*BN*, 175). Since these modalities are irreducible to one another, Sartre rejects Husserl's reduction of being with the result that his phenomenological ontology settles into an ontological dualism.

In this phenomenological reading of for-itself and in-itself, "in-itself" is the objective, inertial character or mode of being of all that appears to the for-itself. Sartre had methodologically committed himself, in *The Transcendence of the Ego*, to the subject/object model with his reading of intentionality. Upon this basis being can appear only as subject or object. The character of in-itself, in this sense, is applicable to all that appears to the self, such as trees, the past, the ego, the Other, qualities. Physical, material objects have the character of in-itself—as all objects—but differ in that they are given through profiles and reveal, across our freedom and action, an experience of resistance and adversity, even of independence: "The internal negation reveals the in-itself as independent, and it is this independence which constitutes in the in-itself its character as a *thing*" (*BN*, 506). All objects have a transcendent modality of in-itself *vis à vis* the self, and are grasped as external to the self. (We will discuss the problem of reflection shortly, the process in which the for-itself becomes an object to itself.) It is peculiar to perceptual objects that they are given with the sense not only of externality but also of independence. From a phenomenological perspective the various characterizations of the in-itself as "inert," "external," "resistant" are characterizations relative to the presence and activity of the for-itself. There is a contingency, a facticity of the modalities of for-itself and in-itself, but any attempt to grasp this facticity presents it as already articulated, differentiated, interpreted. The in-itself is not something hidden behind objective appearance. The appearance "does not point over its shoulder to a true being which would be, for it, absolute. What it is, it is absolutely, for it reveals itself as it is. The phenomenon can be studied and determined as such, for its is *absolutely indicative of itself*" (*BN*, lxvi).

The attempt to trace out a phenomenological reading of for-itself and in-itself has led to a dualism of opposed modalities of being whose intelligibility is reciprocal. This reading began by establishing the ground of Sartre's ontological problematic in Husserl's differentiation of the "heterogeneous" modes of consciousness and object, and in particular of the temporal stream of conscious acts as opposed to the self-sameness of

objects. The resulting dualism has often been likened, even by Sartre, to
Descartes's dualism of *res cogitans* and *res extensa*. The dramatic tension that
Sartre weaves out of the dualism, however, is more reminiscent of
Bergson.[9] Sartre is critical of Bergson for lacking a theory of negation and
a proper theory of reflection, and yet there is a strong resemblance between Bergson's dualism of spontaneity/inertia and Sartre's for-itself and
in-itself. In fact, in *The Transcendence of the Ego*, Sartre characterized the
temporal flux of pre-reflective consciousness as "spontaneity": "This transcendental sphere is a sphere of *absolute* existence, that is to say, a sphere of
pure spontaneity" (*TE*, 96; also 97, 98). He continues to use the characterization throughout *BN*. Both Sartre and Bergson consider the spontaneity of consciousness to be a free creation, Sartre referring to each
moment as "a creation *ex nihilo*," Bergson holding that "each instant is a
fresh endowment . . . the present moment does not find its explanation in
the moment immediately before."[10] Matter for Bergson is equivalent to the
inert, homogeneous, and spatial. Sartre often refers to the in-itself as inert;
in *The Transcendence of the Ego*, he referred to the reified consciousness, the
psychic: "hatred is *inert*" (*TE*, 66). The particular flavor that Sartre gives to
the tension is the flight of the for-itself from inertia. He writes in his *War
Diaries:* "Thus the perpetual flight of the for-itself before the in-itself which
freezes it might be compared to the mobility of a swift stream, which in
intense cold spells may, thanks to the swiftness of the current—escape
freezing" (*WD*, 233). In a characteristic passage from *Being and Nothingness*,
he refers to "a tendency of the . . . in-itself, which is represented by the
pure solid, to fix the liquidity, to absorb the for-itself which ought to
dissolve it" (*BN*, 607). The past and objectification by Other are the prime
instances of the fall of the for-itself toward the condition of in-itself. This
dramatic language used to portray the tension between for-itself and in-
itself marks the point where the phenomenological ontology enters into
relations with the metaphysics of *Being and Nothingness*.

CONSTITUTION AND METAPHYSICS

Our examination of Sartre's early phenomenological works revealed that he
did accept a role for constitution in his phenomenology. Sartre is convinced, however, that there is a radical contingency of being which affects
any attempt to recover and account for it. Consciousness as the "there is" of
being is itself contingent, as is the presence to it of beings other than itself.
All accounts of being presuppose existence, including that of knowers and
knowledge. There was a tendency in his novel *Nausea*, however, to "talk
about" brute factical existence in the absence of words and meaning.[11]
What might be tolerated in a literary experiment such as *Nausea* ought not
to be tolerated in a philosophical study such as *Being and Nothingness*. We do
find several important texts in which Sartre appears well aware of the

problem and in which he appears to reject the notion of an uninterpreted given:

> It is impossible to grasp facticity in its brute nudity, since all that we will find of it is already recovered and freely constructed. (*BN*, 83)

> That brute fact itself is, but apart from the . . . ensemble of meanings which depend on my projects what can it be? This brute existence . . . stands . . . beyond reach. (*BN*, 498)

> It is certain that human reality, by whom the quality of being a world comes to the real, can not encounter the non-human; the very concept of the non-human is man's concept. (*BN*, 533)

> It is in theory possible but in practice impossible to distinguish facticity from the project which constitutes it in situation. (*BN*, 603)

> Every quality of being is all of being; it is the presence of its absolute contingency; it is its indifferent irreducibility. Yet in Part Two we insisted on the inseparability of project and facticity in the simple quality. Thus from the beginning we could not attribute the meaning of a quality to being-*in-itself,* since the 'there is' is already necessary; that is, the nihilating mediation of the for-itself must be there in order for qualities to be there. (*BN*, 603)

These texts forcefully state that, within the context of a phenomenological ontology, the given can only be an articulated, differentiated, interpreted given and that being cannot be "reduced" to the state of a pure given.

It is possible to trace out certain "constitutions" which comprise the "there is" of being. First and foremost is the intentional relationship itself which negates/differentiates being, in its disclosure, into the ontological difference of self-other and the epistemological difference of subject/object. Thus, from the very beginning of Sartre's ontology, what appears objectively does so with the sense of "what is other than self." The negation/differentiation involved in self-consciousness, the "break in being" constitutive of temporality, requires that what appears objectively does so in the context of the past and of future possibility. Then, because the for-itself is a body, ("The body is nothing other than the for-itself," *BN*, 309), the objective appearance is constituted as a "this" (in perception) upon "an undifferentiated ground which is the total perceptive field or the world. The formal structure of this relation of the figure to the ground is therefore necessary" (*BN*, 316). The object, or 'this,' is singled out from the irrelevant indistinction of background by the interest or attention of the for-itself in light of its projects, and thus there is an inevitable moral dimension to the "there is" of being. Finally, while *Being and Nothingness* is practically silent about language, language would itself be a differentiating factor. He does say that "the problem of language is strictly parallel to the problem of body"

(BN, 374), indicating that the for-itself "exists" language and is not outside of it. This would imply that all objective appearances are constituted by the differentiations of language. Within a phenomenological reading of Sartre's ontology, it is possible to correlate the appearance of objects and their relationships and characterizations to these constituting factors of subject/object, temporality, body, project, language. What is interesting about Sartre's theory of constitution is that constitution works by a number of differentiations/negations. But, to reiterate, within the context set by the aforementioned texts on the inseparability of facticity and the differentiating factors, a complete reduction to an undifferentiated given is impossible: "it is impossible to grasp facticity in its brute nudity."

Despite Sartre's own admonitions in this regard, there are texts in which he appears to go beyond his warnings. Right after requiring the necessity of the nihilating mediation of the for-itself in the appearance of qualities, he proceeds to state: "But it is easy to understand in view of these remarks that the meaning of quality in turn indicates something as a re-enforcement of 'there is,' [since we take it as our support in order to surpass the 'there is'] toward being as it is absolutely and in-itself" (BN, 603). Sartre goes on to characterize this surpassing as "a metaphysical effort to escape from our condition so as to pierce through the shell of nothingness about the 'there is' and to penetrate to the pure in-itself" (BN, 603). The references to "pure in-itself" and "being as it is absolutely and in-itself" are to a sense of being which goes beyond the scope of phenomenological methodology. Sartre's own claim is that a phenomenological ontology is grounded in a description of the existent, while metaphysics, going beyond this grounding, provides a hypothetical account. He exemplifies his understanding of ontology and metaphysics when he speculates on the origin of the for-itself and its quest for necessity. From the very beginning of Being and Nothingness, however, Sartre has injected a metaphysical account of being alongside a phenomenological ontology. Recall that, for phenomenological ontology, there is an "inseparability of project and facticity" since it is impossible to grasp "facticity in its brute nudity, since all that we will find of it is already recovered and freely constructed." For phenomenological ontology there can be no sense of "pure being-in-itself." Given Sartre's phenomenological method, being can appear only within the intentional relationship, within the ontological modalities of self/other, and the epistemological dualism of subject/object. When being appears it already has a sense—of self/other, of temporal self-surpassing as opposed to inertial givenness, and identity as bodily oriented. These are "phenomenological senses" of being. From where then does Sartre's metaphysical sense of being arise?

In the process of discussing the relationship between project and facticity, Sartre remarks that "it is in theory possible but in practice impossible to distinguish facticity from the project which constitutes it as situation" (BN, 603). The reference to "in practice" can be taken to mean that from the perspective of phenomenology it is impossible to reduce being to pure facticity since Sartre has admitted the impossibility of encountering the non-human—"the very concept of the non-human is man's concept." The reference to "in theory" can be taken as a reference to metaphysics and indeed Sartre does announce such a *theoretical* account of being, early in *Being and Nothingness* in his discussion of Hegel's *Logic*. Sartre disagrees with Hegel whom he reads as according an oppositional sense to Being and Non-Being. Sartre instead argues that Being and Non-Being are contradictions, with Being having priority over Non-Being. Sartre's modified Hegelian "logic" holds both that "Being is empty *of* all other determination than identity with itself" and that "Negation can not touch the nucleus of being of Being, which is absolute plenitude and positivity" (*BN,* 15). It is this "logic" that allows Sartre to use the metaphysical sense of "pure in-itself" (*BN,* 622) and its "pure nihilation" (*BN,* 617). The logical/metaphysical sense of in-itself and its pure nihilation is established *prior* to the phenomenological account of "the origin of negation." Phenomenologically, the presence of the for-itself as the "there is" of being does lead to a negating/differentiating presence of the for-itself in terms of subjectivity, temporality, body, language, project. But these negating/differentiating factors are specific, not "pure." Correlatively, the in-itself is, as individual, demarcated, given, and identical to itself. The two modalities exist in the tension of spontaneity/inertia. From a phenomenological perspective, the for-itself is a negating/differentiating presence to being. Correlated to this presence is being-as-differentiated; Sartre's metaphysics would take us beneath the intentional relationship to another sense of being, the being prior to its differentiation by the "there is." Sartre insists that "it is the presence of the for-itself which causes the existence of a 'this' . . . it causes a *this* to exist" (*BN,* 180). There is, it is true, a phenomenological sense of the undifferentiated in the Gestaltist notion of figure/background. But this horizontal sense of the undifferentiated is not that of "pure actuality," as Sartre characterizes it when he says that "The in-itself is actuality" (*BN,* 98). The phenomenological sense of the background or horizon is precisely that of context, shifting background, or halo, not of pure actuality. Again, the problem arises: How would one possibly know what "pure being" is, apart from its manifestation to consciousness through the intentional relationship? Sartre's "logic" of pure being and its pure nihilation do not coincide with the concrete phenomenological senses of being and negation that arise out of his description.

Some very pointed criticism has been leveled at *Being and Nothingness* which can be viewed as arising from this strange mix of phenomenology and metaphysics. According to Joseph Fell: "Being-in-itself is at one and the same time determinate and in-determinate. In the terms in which Sartre has posed it, this dilemma is insoluble. *So long as the ground of phenomena is fully actual prior to the intersection of understanding, the phenomenological pro-*

gram cannot be completed."[12] Fell refers to being in-itself (in the sense we have called metaphysical) as the "ground" of phenomena. The question he poses is that of the reality of individual objects and their relationships. If being-in-itself is fully actual and indeterminate before the presence of the for-itself, it cannot become determinate with the presence of the for-itself. And since the for-itself "adds nothing" to the in-itself and its nihilation does not affect being in its "nucleus," what is the reality of the individual in-itself? Granted that Sartre wants to hold that the individual *is* being-in-itself, negated or differented by the for-itself, the for-itself's negation is only metaphysically an "abstraction" that does not touch the nucleus of being.

John Llewelyn approaches the same problem from a similar point of view. He cites a text in which Sartre claims that the for-itself is individuated by being a negation of *"this* in-itself"': There is nothing outside the in-itself except a "reflection [*reflet*] of that nothing which is itself polarized and defined by the in-itself inasmuch as it is precisely the nothingness of *this* in-itself, the individualized nothing which is nothing only because it *is not* the in-itself" (*BN*, 176–77).

But of course Sartre, we have noted, claims that it is the for-itself which creates the existence of the 'this.' Thus Llewelyn comments: "The problem is to understand how on Sartre's analysis the nothing of the for-itself can be individualized if it is individualized in terms of the [individual in-itself and how the in-itself can be individualized if it is individualized in terms of the] for-itself."[13]

These problems arise, of course, because at times Sartre speaks the metaphysical language of "pure in-itself" and "pure nihilation." Sartre himself appears to have these problems on his mind when, in the conclusion of *Being and Nothingness*, he asks: "which shall we call real? . . . the pure in-itself or . . . the in-itself surrounded by that shell of nothingness which we have designated by the name of the for-itself" (*BN*, 622). The difference would appear to be of the greatest significance, for the language about the real as the in-itself surrounded by the for-itself would emphasize the reality of the in-itself as differentiated by the for-itself. It would, in effect, acknowledge the reality of the relation instead of the terms. This metaphysical language would be compatible with the phenomenological ontology which emphasizes the correlation and tension of the modalities. Sartre hesitates to say this, however, because of his view that the for-itself is only an abstraction, metaphysically. The two senses of being, phenomenological and metaphysical, sit side by side in unresolved tension.

REFLECTION, OTHERS, AND AUTHENTICITY

The for-itself can turn its intentional focus upon itself in an act of reflection: "Reflection is the for-itself conscious *of* itself" (*BN*, 150). A circular situation arises wherein the for-itself is both subject and object.

First of all, Sartre stresses that there is "a bond of being" between the reflected-on consciousness and the reflecting consciousness. If there were not, the certainty of the *cogito* would be shattered. Reflection is not an altogether new consciousness that comes upon the scene. "It is not the appearance of a new consciousness directed on the for-itself but an intra-structural modification which the for-itself realizes in itself; it is the for-itself which makes itself exist in the mode reflection reflected-on" (*BN*, 153). Thus, in some sense, "the reflective *is* the reflected-on" (*BN*, 155).

On the other hand, as we have already and consistently observed, objectification implies distantiation and the mode of in-itself. In reflection, the for-itself appears to itself as an object: "the reflected-on must neces-sarily be the *object* for the reflective; and this implies a separation of being" (*BN*, 151). The result is that "it is necessary that the reflective simulta-neously be and not be the reflected-on" (*BN*, 151). The relation of the for-itself to itself in reflection is that of subject/object, but is not the same type of relation as that of the for-itself to an object other than itself. Sartre marks this difference by referring to the reflected-on as a "quasi object." The for-itself as reflected-on is not wholly external to the for-itself reflecting (be-cause of the "bond of being" required by the demand of the certitude of the *cogito*), and so the "negation is not entirely realized. It does not detach itself completely from the reflected-on" (*BN*, 155).

Sartre particularly stresses throughout the discussion of reflection that "there can be no question . . . of a total identification" (*BN*, 151). Thus, reflection itself reflects the ambiguity of the pre-reflective *cogito*. On the pre-reflective level, consciousness attains itself (is "present to" itself) only as escaping from itself (is present to what is other than itself). There is a continual "break in being," which precludes self-identity. Reflection, too, cannot totally identify with the reflected-on, since reflection is non-posi-tionally present to itself as it intends its object, the reflected-on. Thus the self remains elusive to itself, can never gain hold of itself completely.

There can intervene an impure reflection, which tries to remedy this elusiveness and break the tension and ambiguity that mark the relation between reflecting and reflected-on. Impure reflection attempts to consider the reflected-on as an object that the reflecting either totally *is* or totally *is not*. This would allow the reflecting consciousness to either recover or repudiate the reflected-on. In this sense the discussion of the impure reflection mirrors Sartre's discussion of bad faith, which is an attempt to break the tension in existence between transcendence (freedom) and fac-ticity (being-in-the world). Human existence as a fact is always given a meaning (interpreted) through a free project. Thus, human existence defines itself. The waiter who considers himself *to be* a waiter as a fixed in-itself and the homosexual who refuses to admit his or her self-definition are inauthentic, hiding from themselves either freedom or facticity respec-tively. Thus Sartre's position that "it is necessary that the reflective simultaneously be and not be the reflected-on" parallels his definition of human reality as "a being which is what it is not and is not what it is." There is a similar parallel when he discusses the motivations for impure reflection and bad faith.

Impure reflection arises out of the natural inclination of reflection as such to "recover itself." "Reflection [reflexion] remains for the for-itself a permanent possibility, an attempt to recover being" (*BN*, 153). The "recovery" would be to gather itself together so as to found itself: "reflection is a second effort by the for-itself to found itself: that is, *to be for itself what it is*" (*BN*, 153). Reflection is a "second effort" as, supposedly, bad faith is a first effort. The "recovery" aimed at in bad faith is the ontological self-foundation or project of being God or necessary being, the discussion of which in *Being and Nothingness* has received so much attention. By an "a priori" analysis of the pre-reflective *cogito*, Sartre establishes that, since the pre-reflective consciousness is present to self, it *lacks* identity with itself, and that it *desires* identity with itself. Human *action* thus is viewed as aiming at the ideal *value* of achieving the identity of self while being the self-conscious (and free) choice of self. This "necessary" being would both *be* a self and make itself be that self. Thus Sartre "explains" the "flight" behavior he had disclosed in *The Transcendence of the Ego* and had elaborated in an early section of *Being and Nothingness*. Under the desire to be necessary the for-itself can use its objectified self to try to recover and fix its perpetual elusiveness to itself, constituted by the break in being. Under the desire to be necessary, the human existent can lie to itself about its ambiguous constitution of freedom/facticity, try to consider itself as a fixed, finished being, and avoid responsibility for its continuous self-definition.

To counter impure reflection and offer the possibility of "deliverance," Sartre insists on the possibility of a "pure reflection." He had indicated its possibility, we have seen, in *The Transcendence of the Ego* and he continues to do so in *Being and Nothingness*. "Only a *pure* reflective consciousness can discover the for-itself reflected on in its reality" (*BN*, 163). Pure reflection can effect upon itself a "katharsis" and as a result, in its thematization of the pre-reflective, take cognizance of the "break in being," of the non-positional presence to self. He is not explicit about pure reflection in *Being and Nothingness* for he continually reminds us that "this is not the place to describe the motivation and structure of the katharis" (*BN*, 160). Beyond holding that in pure reflection the self is grasped as "break in being" (temporality) and as "having to be," that is, self-interpretive, not much is offered. Even, as we shall see, when he takes up the issue directly in his *Cahiers*, he will not add much more precision.

Once more there is a parallel between the level of reflection and that of existence. Just as a pure reflection is possible, so is a "conversion" from bad faith to authenticity. Following the discussions of individual bad faith and social bad faith (in "Concrete Relation with Other," *BN*) there appear footnotes which clearly indicate the possibility of this conversion.

> If it is indifferent whether one is in good or in bad faith, because good faith slides to the very origin of the project of good faith, that does not mean that we can not radically escape bad faith. But this supposes a self-recovery of being which was previously corrupted. This self-recovery we shall call authenticity, the description of which has no place here. (*BN*, 70)

> These considerations do not exclude the possibility of an ethics of deliverance and salvation. But this can be achieved only after a radical conversion which we can not discuss here. (*BN*, 412)

The key to this conversion is the rejection by reflective consciousness of the desire to be God. Sartre raises this possibility explicitly in the brief discussion of play, which is an activity that has for its end the exercise of freedom. Such a project is "radically different" from the project of losing oneself to gain the ideal of necessary being.

> It would be necessary to explain in full detail its relations with the project of being-God, which has appeared to us as the deep-seated structure of human reality. But such a study can not be made here; it belongs rather to an *Ethics* and it supposes that there has been a preliminary definition of nature and the role of purifying reflection (our descriptions have hitherto aimed only at *accessory* reflection). (*BN*, 581)

Early in *Being and Nothingness,* Sartre had indicated that pure reflection would function as Husserl's epoché, snatching consciousness from an apparent obsession with its objects: "only reflective consciousness can be dissociated from what is posited by the consciousness reflected-on. It is only in the reflective level that we can attempt an 'ἐποχή, a putting between parentheses, only there that we can refuse what Husserl calls the *mitmachen*" (*BN*, 75). Sartre understands this *mitmachen* to be a complicity with the natural attitude overcomable by reduction. The "natural" desire to be necessary which haunts pre-reflective existence remains, but is "bracketed." The reflective consciousness need not participate in it. Instead, as Sartre suggests in the last line of *Being and Nothingness*, reflective consciousness can accept the "break in being," its own failure to be, as a positive sense of freedom itself: "A freedom which wills itself freedom is in fact a being-which-is-not-what-it-is and which is what it is not, and which chooses as the ideal of being, being what it is-not and not-being what it is" (*BN*, 627). The *Cahiers* confirms this movement beyond impure reflection and bad faith. Sartre establishes from the beginning "the very fact that *Being and Nothingness* is an ontology prior to conversion supposes that a conversion is necessary and consequently there is a natural attitude" (*C*, 13). He reiterates that pure reflection acts as a phenomenological epoché: "reflection holds spontaneity between parentheses, in suspense, without removing its affirmative force, as the phenomenological epoché or non-accessory reflection does not at all prevent the affirmation of the reality of the world in the natural attitude" (*C*, 12; see also *C*, 490). This sets up the conversion from aiming at necessary being ("authenticity consists in refusing the quest for being," *C*, 492) and in living with the tension of the "break in being" ("authenticity will consist in maintaining the tension," *C* 492). The movement from impure reflection to pure and from bad faith to authenticity in the for-itself's relation to itself necessarily spills over into its relations with Others.

We have observed the failure of the for-itself to recover, in identity, its own objectified image of itself. In the course of discussing this failure, Sartre observes parenthetically: "In order for the consciousness reflected-on to be 'viewed from without' and in order for reflection to be able to orient itself in relation to it, it would be necessary that the reflective should not be the reflected-on in the mode of not-being what it is not: this scissiparity will be realized only in existence *for-others*" (*BN*, 155). In our discussion of the in-itself we observed that the objectified Other is grasped in the mode of the in-itself. Even as projecting itself toward goals, the Other is a "transcendence transcended." My access to the Other is through the Other's body: "The body of the Other is given to me as the pure in-itself of his being an in-itself among in-itselfs and one which I surpass toward my possibilities" (*BN*, 343). To reiterate, the Other's very surpassing of identity is fixed into the mode of the in-itself: "The Other's for-itself wrenches itself away from this contingency and perpetually surpasses it. But insofar as I transcend the Other's transcendence, I fix it. It is no longer a recourse against facticity" (*BN*, 343).

The Other as subjectivity cannot, by definition, be given to me as an appearance, for this would cast the Other into objectivity. The other side of the coin, of course, is that the Other can look at me, fixing me into the mode of the in-itself. It is through my experience of my objectivity for the Other that I encounter the Other as a subject: "With the appearance of the Other's look I experience the revelation of my being-as-object; that is, of my transcendence transcended" (*BN*, 351). This occurs because I am an objectified body. The body which I exist for myself becomes cast into the dimension of the in-itself under the gaze of the Other.

> The shock of the encounter with the Other is for me a revelation in emptiness of the existence of my body outside as an in-itself for the Other. Thus my body is not given merely as that which is purely and simply lived; rather this 'lived experience' becomes—in and through the contingent, absolute fact of the Other's existence—extended outside in a dimension of flight which escapes me. (*BN*, 352)

This type of in-itself which I am for the Other is quite different from the state of quasi-objectivity that I am for myself through reflection. When I reflect upon myself, I am a subject and remain so in relation to myself, even when I look at myself in a mirror. But when I am looked at by the Other, my very subjectivity, the break in being, is fixed in the in-itself and I recognize this: "Shame reveals to me that I *am* this being, not in the mode of 'was' or of 'having to be' but *in-itself*" (*BN*, 262). Due to the Other I am transformed into the mode of the in-itself, a mode radically different from my being for myself: "my being-as-object or being-for-others is profoundly different from my being-for-myself" (*BN*, 273). "My transcendence becomes . . . a purely established transcendence, a given-transcendence" (*BN*, 262).

The metamorphosis is depicted as shameful, degrading. The reason for this is, of course, that "before conversion" human reality is caught in the throes of (haunted by) the desire to be God (necessary being) and to such a consciousness the existence of the Other is a scandal. The Other reveals to me that I am just a point of view upon the world, and that I am no longer master. I am vulnerable. My own situation for me disappears as I experience myself being surpassed by the Other toward his or her possibles: "But if instrumentality is defined as the fact of 'being able to be surpassed towards ——, then my very possibility becomes an instrumentality" (*BN*, 264). This crushing experience can motivate the two different inauthentic attitudes toward the Other portrayed in "Concrete Relations with Others," and in his play *No Exit*. On the one hand, insofar as the Other "founds" me as in-itself, I can attempt to possess the Other's subjectivity which founds me (love) or attempt to lose myself in my objectivity (masochism). Or, on the other hand, I can attempt to eradicate the subjectivity of the Other, either by ignoring it (indifference) or by assuming my subjectivity, in an attempt to control the Other's subjectivity through his or her objectivity (sexual desire, sadism). But these inauthentic manoeuvers are doomed to fail. Only a circle of vain attempts to be pure subject or pure object exists. Escape can only come from rejecting the desire to be God. Thus Others are not so much "hell" as is the pursuit of necessity: "The pursuit of Being, that is hell" (*C*, 42). The Other who objectifies me is not my enemy nor is objectification a degradation once the conversion has been effected: "through the Other I become an object. And this is, *in itself*, in no way a danger or disgrace. That would come about only if the Other refused *also* to recognize freedom in me" (*C*, 515). Thus, the *Cahiers* depicts relationships in quite a different way from *Being and Nothingness:* mutual recognition and respect, generosity and cooperation.

Perhaps the primary effect of the conversion is the acceptance of contingency-facticity: "the free acceptance of contingency and finitude" (*C*, 562). Instead of *nausea*, there appears "joy" over the "gift" of existing

(C 486, 502, 570). There is also acceptance of freedom, as the authentic human reality "recovers itself in its existential dimension of choice" (C, 373) and makes as goal in life not necessary being, but its own freedom: "pure reflection is . . . the setting up of a freedom which takes itself as its goal" (C, 578). The relation of self to Other, after conversion, "is neither appropriation nor identification" (C, 500). Rather the for-itself accepts its "loss of self" in intentionality as the price for the revelation of what is other than itself (C, 510–12).

The *Cahiers*, while not published by Sartre, can be considered the companion volume promised at the end of *Being and Nothingness*. Together, in sharing the ontology of self-Other and epistemology of subject/object, they comprise the phase of his work before the turn toward dialectic, a turn that will come to challenge the very foundation of *Being and Nothingness* and the *Cahiers*. For the present, however, it should be clear from this discussion of reflection, alterity, and authenticity that the relations between self and self, self and Other, subject and object, can be characterized from the radically different perspectives of the desire for necessity and conversion.

FROM PRE-REFLECTIVE TO REFLECTIVE

In presenting the in-itself, for-itself, and for-Others, Sartre brings into play three types of consciousness: pre-reflective, reflective (impure), and reflective (pure). He consistently gives the pre-reflective ontological priority over the reflective since the latter could not exist without the former. Problems arise, however, when he discusses the epistemological relationships among these levels of consciousness.

Several years after the publication of *Being and Nothingness*, Sartre spoke on the topic "Self-Consciousness and Self-Knowledge" before the French Philosophical Society. In the course of the question period Sartre put to himself the following question: "Is it possible to pass from immediate consciousness to pure reflection?" He replied: "I know nothing about it. Perhaps one can achieve it after the exercise of pure reflection, but I could not say *a priori* that a being living on the level of pure immediacy is capable of pure reflection."[14] In *Being and Nothingness*, bad faith, as a flight from freedom, presupposes its knowledge. Thus, prior to discussing bad faith, Sartre speaks of an anguished grasp of oneself as "totally free" and the source of all meaning and value. Bad faith may well be the "immediate behavior with respect to freedom" (BN, 40), but it would appear that at least a momentary flash of pure reflection grounds its possibility.[15] By the time he worked on the *Cahiers*, however, his mind was made up: "Reflection arises originally as accessory [*complice*]. . . . Pure reflection is necessarily posterior to impure reflection" (C, 18). Sartre accompanies this by holding that bad faith arises naturally before authenticity: "I do not deny that there is a nature, that is to say, one begins by flight and the inauthentic" (C, 13).

The uncharacteristic use of "nature" in this context refers to the desire to be necessary which haunts pre-reflective consciousness. The implication is that impure reflection and bad faith are tied together in a circular relation. As long as one is under the spell of the desire for necessity, reflection will be accomplice to this desire.

If pure reflection is subsequent to impure, there remains the question of how consciousness is aware that it is totally free, which is the necessary condition for flight behavior. One possible explanation is to push the issue on to the pre-reflective consciousness. We have already had occasion to observe that from its first presentation in *The Transcendence of the Ego* the pre-reflective consciousness has been an ambiguous phenomenon. Jean Hyppolite, who was present when Sartre spoke to the French Philosophical Society, was quick to direct his comment to this point.

> You have proposed a kind of intermediate stage which is not purely dialectical between the immediacy of the life and mediation, the stage which Hegel introduces under the form of negativity, and you have introduced this intermediary term which characterizes human reality; this intermediary pre-reflective term is formulated sometimes as immediacy . . . ; afterwards you began to see a mediating quality in it because it includes within it presence to itself as well as absence from itself.[16]

Sartre's response illustrates the ambiguity of his view of the pre-reflective: "the immediacy of consciousness is an immediate which is not entirely an immediate, while being it."[17] We have already observed that there is a sense of self and a sense of being a subject that is necessarily implied in the ontological distinction self/other and the epistemological distinction subject/object. For example, Sartre writes of the for-itself: "this nothingness is not anything except human reality apprehending itself as excluded from being and perpetually beyond being" (*BN*, 181).[18] Again, the possibility of the recovery of my subjectivity in the face of the Look of the Other is the comprehension of my self: "this implicit comprehension is nothing other than the consciousness (of) my 'being myself' " (*BN*, 289). He refers on another occasion to "the consciousness (of) my free spontaneity" (*BN*, 287).

The comprehension of self and freedom is an important theme in the *Cahiers*. He asks how the oppressed know that they are free, and replies:

> First, because they attain themselves immediately, by non-thetic self-consciousness, which envelops an ontological comprehension of existence as absolute subjectivity. They know themselves directly as the foundation of every system of alienation. It is not fear and work which will give self-consciousness to the slave. It is already there. It is not a virtuality but the very mode of existing and the original condition. . . . There is in all human activity a comprehension of the human condition and of freedom. (*C*, 488)

He indicates that bad faith and authenticity take their source in the "non-thetic consciousness that freedom has of itself" (*C*, 578). Against all attempts to reduce consciousness to a thing there persists "the contestation of non-thetic self-consciousness" (*C*, 401). In these cases pre-reflective self-consciousness is treated as an inescapable lucidity of freedom to itself.

Yet Sartre does on occasion speak of a consciousness which lives as if in a pure immediate.

> For human reality, being-in-the-world means radically to lose oneself in the world through the very revelation which causes there to be a world. (*BN*, 200)

> Thus in what we shall call the world of the immediate, [which delivers itself to our reflective consciousness,] we do not first appear to ourselves, to be thrown subsequently into enterprises. Our being is immediately in situation, that is, it arises in enterprises and knows itself first insofar as it is reflected in these enterprises. (*BN*, 39)

In describing this immediate consciousness, he claims that "we do not first appear to ourselves," indicating thereby that the sense of self and its difference from objects so clearly present in the texts on the pre-reflective *cogito* is displaced. This "immediate consciousness" would understand itself hermeneutically through language, culture, etc. The waffling over pre-reflective consciousness as immediacy and presence to self pointed out by Hyppolite is on the mark. When one begins to sort out these variously depicted types of consciousness it is apparent that there are two different versions of pre-reflective consciousness (immediacy and pre-reflective *cogito*) and two different types of reflection (impure and pure). The discrepancies and lack of coordination among them follow from Sartre's lack of a theory of the development of consciousness. Birth and death are factical beginning and end with no bearing upon the understanding of life in between. The for-itself appears on the scene as a highly self-conscious individual and that is that. The for-itself's heightened sense of individuality, freedom, and opposition to nature are not related to either history or culture or personal life history. As his paradigm is that of the *cogito*, the epistemological basis for individuality, freedom, negativity, is the reflexive nature of consciousness itself. The assumption of *Being and Nothingness* and his literature of that period is that there are only two sorts of people, those in bad faith and those who are authentic, and both types know that they are totally free.

From the perspective of the *cogito*, Sartre rejects Heidegger's hermeneutical theory of self-understanding. Sartre's discourse of subjectivity and objectivity represents hermeneutics as an attempt to translate subjectivity into objectivity. Accessible only to itself, subjectivity is incommensurable with any objectification of itself. Sartre makes it clear in *Being and Nothingness* and in the *Cahiers* that it is bad faith, inauthentic, for consciousness to understand itself in terms of the world. In *Being and Nothingness* Sartre refers to "the circuit of selfness," by which he means that the self and world are correlated such that the world is constituted by the self's projects and the self's possibilities are made known by the world. For Sartre, however, this (hermeneutical) circularity must be transcended: "the possibility of positing the problem of meaning on this level does not exist. We work to live and we live to work. The question of the *meaning* of the totality 'life-work'—'why do I work, I who am living? Why live if it is in order to work?'—this can be posited only on the reflective level since it implies a self-discovery on the part of the for-itself" (*BN*, 201). Hermeneutical self-understanding is an impure reflection. Pure reflection reveals the self as the source of meaning, not as defined by any meaning. Pure reflection is autonomy over meaning; impure reflection is heteronomy. The self eludes meaning, slips through its categories, conceptions, etc., to stand face to face with meaning. *Meaning* appears as outside, secreted by the for-itself, and stands as an object incommensurable with the spontaneity of the for-itself.

Thus, Sartre claims that meaning (and language) is an issue of being-for-Others: "I cannot confer on myself any quality without mediation or an objectifying power which is not my own power and which I can neither pretend nor forge. Of course this has been said before; it was said a long time ago that the Other teaches me who I am" (*BN*, 274). But, of course, from the vantage point of subjectivity, "I am not what I am." While I recognize that I *am* for the Other and that the Other can characterize me, justly, as this or that, *for-myself* I cannot be this or that. For myself I am the elusive self, the "break-in-being." Thus, quite often in *Being and Nothingness* the for-itself is given as "knowing" itself by way of a *via negativa*—as not an object—quantity, quality etc. At other times the for-itself, by reason of its non-positional self-consciousness, "knows that it knows," "knows that it believes," "knows that it has pleasure." In any case the two sources of self-knowledge in *Being and Nothingness*, from the for-itself itself and from its being-for-Others, offer incompatible views of the self.

This position is reiterated in the *Cahiers:* "I am then with two types of consciousness: the one, mediated, which comes to me through the Other; the Other which comes to me through myself. Between these knowledges no synthesis is possible since one resides in the Other and one in me" (*C*, 466–67). The unsynthesizable dualism between these types of self-knowledge thus reflects similar irreconcilable bifications already touched upon such as subject/object, pre-reflective/reflective, bad faith/authenticity. We shall soon see the dual, and exclusory, forms of self-knowledge as well as these other dualisms and the *cogito* paradigm itself from which they arise be put to the test when Sartre discovers, under the force of circumstances, the conditioned consciousness. The facticity of birth and cultural and historical place will emerge from the anonymity of being the background for the power of consciousness to impel a discourse of the *formation* of consciousness.

While *Being and Nothingness* is not the ethics or politics promised at the end of *The Transcendence of the Ego,* it would appear that its conclusions are basic to any attempt to construct an ethics and politics and in this regard *Being and Nothingness* takes us well beyond the lesson of *The Transcendence of the Ego.* The ontology of *Being and Nothingness* centers on the self/otherness difference, translating into ontological vocabulary the epistemological distinction of subject/object evident in the early works as Sartre's principal methodological tool. As Sartre defines these terms, self/otherness and subject/object in *Being and Nothingness* are exclusory. The drive to unite these terms (the passion of Western thought), to find some ultimate intelligibility and necessity in a unitary notion of Being, is futile and must be abandoned. An ethics and politics of human finitude would require a recognition of the insuperable difference between self and otherness. Instead of an attempt to appropriate or assimilate otherness to self or vice versa, both must accept their exclusory difference. We have seen that Sartre attempts to express this already in the *Cahiers.* The project, however, is burdened with the Kantian and Hegelian language he uses to express insights that do not really fit the context of the thought of either of these philosophers. Thus, in the *Cahiers,* the moral and political project does not get properly formulated. The project was left unfinished, postponed, until he could assimilate into the established pattern of his thought his newly acquired social and historical experiences. What occurred was that these new experiences put the task of moral and political thought, as well as ontology, into a new light, and under intense pressure to accommodate them.

THREE

The Intrusion of Otherness

Sartre's theory of consciousness has culminated in his version of the existential project, the centerpiece of the thesis of the power of consciousness. Beyond determination by cause, motive, or object, the project is the contingent and unjustifiable foundation of meaning and value. The ontological structure of being-for-itself displayed the autonomy of the project by referring it to the being of human reality, which is a continual wrenching away or rupture from what is other than itself. As a result, human reality "is wholly and forever free or . . . is not free at all" (BN, 441).

The philosophy of the existential project and radical freedom was formulated prior to World War II, or at least up to and including the "phony war" phase of that World War. On just about every occasion given him since then to comment on his works, Sartre has informed the world how he has *changed* since that time, primarily because of his experiences during the war years. "It was the war which shattered the worn structures of our thought—War, Opposition, Resistance, the years which followed" (SM, 20). In his interview of 1969, "The Itinerary of a Thought," he summed up why his outlook "changed so fundamentally": "A simple formula would be to say that life taught me *la force des choses*—the power of circumstances" (BEMIT, 33). Under the impact of his insight into the force of circumstances, Sartre tells us in the interview, he came to see that some of his earlier views had, at least, to be toned down.

> For my state of mind during those years, I think that the first plays I wrote are very symptomatic: I called them a 'theatre of freedom.' The other day I reread a prefatory note of mine to a collection of these plays—*Les Mouches, Huis Clos* and others—and was truly scandalized. I had written: "whatever the circumstances, and wherever the site, a man is always free to choose to be a traitor or resist. . . ." When I read this, I said to myself it's incredible, I actually believed that! (BEMIT, 33–34)

In analyzing how such an incredibility could occur, he states that "*L'Être et Le Néant* traced an interior experience, without any coordination with the exterior experience of a petty-bourgeois intellectual" (BEMIT, 35), thereby acknowledging that he is not simply backing off from a former case of exaggerated writing but that something was conceptually inadequate. From

41

the perspective of 1969 he reconsiders one of his original bifurcations: "Thus, in *L'Être et Le Néant,* what you could call 'subjectivity' is not what it would be for me now. But 'subjectivity' and 'objectivity' seem to me entirely useless notions today, anyway" *(BEMIT,* 35). On the face of it, this is a bold statement since subjectivity served as a primary concept in his existential ontology. The question inevitably arises about the fate of the concepts that cluster about it.

For the early Sartre psychology and philosophy were the same, and he looked upon his work as laying the foundation of a new psychology. "Interior experience" could be called its subject matter and phenomenological reflection its method. The result was the thesis of the power of consciousness in the theory of the existential project. Despite the emphasis Sartre puts on how much he has since changed, he unflinchingly continues to be committed to human freedom and he refuses to reduce human beings to the level of things. It is clear, however, that his conception of freedom has changed—"There's no question that there is some basic change in the concept of freedom," he announced in the film *Sartre by Himself.* Given the systematic presentation he has made of his previous conception of freedom, it is certain that any "basic change" to freedom will affect other related concepts. The question arises regarding the extent to which his ontology can support these changes. Specifically, much depends upon what Sartre understands to be the "co-ordination" of interior and exterior—for our purposes, the power of consciousness and the force of circumstances. Our task then is to track down the changes in Sartre's understanding of the human condition that result from his newly acquired appreciation of the force of circumstances and to measure them against his previous work. We will begin by examining several major texts in which the force of circumstances finds a voice and takes on some initial articulation. These texts are: the inaugural editorial in *Les Temps Modernes, Saint Genet: Actor and Martyr, The Communists and Peace,* and *The Words.*

"PRESENTATION" TO *LES TEMPS MODERNES*

Sartre's "presentation," or inaugural editorial, in the first issue of *Les Temps Modernes* in 1945 differs markedly in attitude and vocabulary from his preceding work. He insists upon the "social function" of literature, a theme upon which he will soon expand in *What Is Literature?.* The notion of situation, present in *Being and Nothingness* as the ever-present background for freedom, is now focused upon and charged with a weightiness it was not allotted in the ontology. "The writer is *situated* in his time." Situatedness is reflected principally in the *class* to which the writer belongs. The bourgeoisie have invented the myth of pure art, art for art's sake, which is an escape from addressing real issues in the course of which the writer's own status in a hierarchically divided society would come to the fore. The myth of pure art is allied to the cult of the beautiful and the project of attaining immortality ("Immortality is a terrible alibi"), all of which constitute retreats into the imaginary.

Sartre aims to address directly the issues of present reality. Since literature always bears the stamp of its time, a responsible literature assumes its time, taking on its problems. Moreover, there is a commitment, beyond mere analysis, to action: "our intention is to participate in bringing forth certain changes in our society. By this we do not mean a change in the souls. . . . We side with those who want to change both the social condition of man and his conception of himself" (*LTM*, 435). This is to be carried out by rejecting "relativism" and embracing unashamedly the value of freedom: "the person is nothing else but his freedom" (*LTM*, 441).

Freedom finds an important place in the "Presentation," to be sure, but what is new in the discussion of situatedness is the recognition of and emphasis upon the phenomenon of social conditioning. For example, Sartre refers to "factors which constitute" a human being and of the "situations which condition . . . totally": "Totally conditioned by his class, his salary, the nature of his work, conditioned even to his feelings, his thoughts . . . a worker cannot live as a bourgeois; in the social organization of today, he must suffer to the end his condition of salaried worker; no escape is possible" (*LTM*, 441). To belong to a class is to live and manifest a specific situation in a way that defines one holistically: "we deny the individual's origin, class, milieu, nation, to be mere concurrents in his sentimental life. On the contrary, we think that every affection, as any other form of his psychic life, *manifests* his social situation" (*LTM*, 438).

Echoing his call for a change in "self-conception," Sartre sees a need for a "synthetic anthropology" to replace the "analytic turn of mind" which defines bourgeois mentality, and "blinds one from collective realities." For the bourgeois, human beings are atoms, solitary individuals whose only concept of fraternity is that of "one pea in a can of peas: he is all round, closed within himself, incommunicable" (*LTM* 436). Human beings are "juxtaposed" and have no true unity. Relations are "external," "passive." Analytical thought cannot conceive "solidarity of class or action." This bourgeois mentality is motivated by political and economic interest. Since each human molecule has a nature that makes it equal to other human molecules, there is no need for action to make them equal. In addition, liberal individualism is a tactic of admitting formal rights, such as voting, "to isolate men in favor of the privileged classes." According to the synthetic view championed by Sartre, people have to be *liberated* by effecting changes of social structure, which are the conditions for a real freedom. He ends by referring to an individual whose situation allows only for a choice of life or death: "it is this free man who must be *delivered*, by widening his possibilities of choice. In certain situations, there is only room for one alternative, one term of which is death. It must be so that man can choose life, in any circumstances" (*LTM*, 441).

While he does not advert to it, throughout the entire piece Sartre is both renouncing and sharply modifying positions he had earlier held. During the period he wrote *Nausea*, Sartre himself was under the spell of achieving immortality. Then, when he argues in *Being and Nothingness* that one is either totally free or totally determined, he sounds very much like the bourgeois whose attitude toward equality he condemns. After all, if human beings are already free, what is the sense of taking action to liberate them? Furthermore, Sartre in his "Presentation" cynically denigrates those who would merely intend to produce "a change in the souls." Yet is this not a fitting description of his own notion of a "radical conversion" of the individual to authenticity in *Being and Nothingness*? Finally, and this deserves our further consideration, what basis was there in his earlier writings for lecturing his readers now on "conditioning" and "solidarity"?

The notion of conditioning would find its general intelligibility in *Being and Nothingness* in the discussion of situatedness and facticity. Whenever he wishes to distance himself from idealism, Sartre claims as his own Heidegger's "being-in-the-world." We have noted, however, that in *Being and Nothingness* texts that stress the power of consciousness over its situation are predominant. In fact, freedom is regularly conceived of as the capacity to "escape" and "negate" its situation through an "unjustifiable" choice. "It is impossible for objects to act upon consciousness," and so "choice is always unconditioned" (*BN*, 442, 479). Most often, situation and facticity serve as the necessary but neutral backdrop to freedom's power. Perhaps the discussions in *Being and Nothingness* of the relationship between freedom and facticity that bear most closely on the issues raised by Sartre in his "Presentation" are those carried on under the heading "My Fellowman," and the "*Us* Object" and "*We* Subject":

> To live in a world haunted by my fellowman is not only to be able to encounter the Other at every turn of the road; it is also to find myself engaged in a world in which instrumental-complexes can have a meaning which my free project has not first given to them. It means also that in the midst of this world *already* provided with meaning I meet with a meaning which is *mine* and which I have not given to myself, which I discover that I "possess already." (*BN*, 509–10)

This text of "My Fellowman," which opens discussion, shows promise of broaching the issue of social conditioning. That possibility deepens when a short time later we find reference to "birth" and "class."

> Now it is evident that although my belonging to a particular class or nation does not derive from my facticity as an ontological structure of my for-itself, my factual existence—i.e., my birth and my place—involves my apprehension

of the world and of myself through certain techniques. Now these techniques which I have not chosen confer on the world its meanings. It appears that it is no longer I who decide in terms of my ends whether the world appears to me with the simple, well-marked oppositions of the 'proletarian' universe or with the innumerable interwoven nuances of the 'bourgeois' world. I am not only thrown face to face with the brute existent. I am thrown into a worker's world, a French world, a world of Lorraine or the South, which offers me its meanings without my having done anything to disclose them. (*BN*, 514)

Facticity, whether of things, Others, or myself, is never grasped in its nudity but through the mediation of a highly structured world. The thrust of this compilation of factors in the situation leads Sartre to admit that "the for-itself is free but *in condition,* and it is the relation of this condition to freedom that we are trying to define by making clear the meaning of the situation" (*BN*, 514). The important question then is "the relation" of freedom and condition, particularly what effect the mediation of structures has on freedom. Sartre never does address that issue, however. He defensively contends that the for-itself chooses itself "beyond" condition: "Each for-itself, in fact, is a for-itself only by choosing itself beyond nationality and race. . . . This 'beyond' is enough to assure its total independence in relation to the structures which it surpasses; but the fact remains that it constitutes itself as *beyond* in relation to *these* particular structures" (*BN*, 520). Sartre simply restates the problem, juxtaposing the terms "beyond" and "these particular structures" without penetrating into the relationship itself. He does claim that the for-itself "interiorizes" techniques, but in doing so it is apparently unaffected by them: "The technique . . . because it is interiorized, *loses its character as a technique* and is integrated purely and simply in the free surpassing of the given toward ends" (*BN*, 523; emphasis added). Sartre's entire focus remains on freedom with the insistence that there would be no situation, no meaning at all, no structures, without freedom. A situation is *for* consciousness and open to the imposition of meaning by consciousness. In the course of his defense of freedom in the face of facticity, he provides an interesting example, the Jew in occupied France. The for-itself becomes a "Jew" in the eyes of Others, insofar as that appellation has meaning. In occupied France, being a Jew meant something dangerous. There are prohibitions. Jews can or cannot do certain things under pain of death. This would appear to limit the freedom of the for-itself. Sartre points out, however, that a "prohibition can have meaning only on and through the foundation of my free choice" (*BN*, 525). I can choose to disobey or grant a "coercive value" to the prohibition, depending upon "whether under any circumstances I prefer life to death." Sartre's "Presentation," it will be recalled, ended with a similar example, a person in a life-or-death situation. Sartre's attitude on that later occasion, however, is that "it is this free man who must be *delivered,* by widening his possibilities of choice." The implication for his previous example is that the Jew could be *freer* if his situation offered more opportunities. The implication of the position taken in the "Presentation" is that choice and situation are in a closer relation than was understood to be the case in *Being and Nothingness,* and in particular that possibility has an objective meaning. One can now appreciate why Sartre later found "incredible" some of the earlier claims he had made about freedom. It also explains to some degree why Sartre was so stoical in relation to politics in *Being and Nothingness* as opposed to his activism in the "Presentation."

Sartre's recognition of "solidarity" and his repudiation of bourgeois liberalism's individualism is curious in the light of what little he had to say about the social in *Being and Nothingness.* While he had admitted that Heidegger's *mitsein* is "a sort of ontological solidarity," he rejected the notion: "Heidegger's being-with is not the clear and distinct position of an individual confronting another individual" *(BN,* 246). The confrontational position is, for Sartre, original, since the very being of the for-itself is an internal negation of the Other, and vice versa: "the negation which constitutes the Other is direct, internal, and reciprocal" *(BN,* 238). Thus, "human reality at the very heart of its *ekstases* remains alone" *(BN,* 240). The result, for social ontology, is pessimistic: "the multiplicity of consciousness is on principle unsurpassable" *(BN,* 244).

There is a sense of solidarity not on the basis of subjectivity but on that of objectivity, which is described in the phenomenon of the *Us,* or "community alienation" *(BN,* 415). "It is possible," he writes, "for some sort of plurality of individuals to experience itself as *Us*" *(BN,* 420). The dyadic, face to face, subject/object relation of one consciousness to another can be abruptly altered by the appearance on the scene of a Third. The Third, by looking at the Other and me, causes *Us* to share the common condition of being-objects-for-It. Here a form of solidarity appears: "I suddenly experience the existence of an objective situation-form in the world of the Third in which the Other and I shall figure as *equivalent* structures in *solidarity* with each other" *(BN,* 418). On this basis Sartre attempted to make class consciousness intelligible. Class consciousness is presented as "the assuming of a particular *Us*" *(BN,* 420). The role of the Third is pivotal in forging the unity of a class—not material things or structures of the world, but the Look of the Third:

> The "master," the "feudal lord," the "bourgeois," the "capitalist" all appear not only as powerful people who command but in addition and above all as *Thirds;* that is, as those who are outside the oppressed community and for whom this community exists. . . . They cause it to be born by their look. . . . Thus the oppressed class finds its unity in the knowledge which the oppressing class has of it. *(BN,* 421)

The "bond" among the oppressed according to this account is purely external and disappears with the disappearance of the Third.

The idea of a common subjectivity, or *We*, is dismissed as having only a psychological reality. The *We* would comprise a "lateral" awareness since a "frontal" awareness would by definition create a subject/object situation, implicating internal negation. There are *We* type experiences generated by participating in common activities, but even in this case there is no guarantee that all participants share the same experience of being-with: "the experience of the *We* subject is a pure psychological subjective event in a single consciousness" (*BN*, 425).

Given this portrayal of social reality in *Being and Nothingness* it is surprising to see the bitterness with which Sartre, in his "Presentation," repudiates bourgeois liberalism and its "analytic" bias in approaching social phenomena. If liberalism only "juxtaposed" individuals, what did *Being and Nothingness* offer that went beyond that? Furthermore, with its conception of subjectivity as negation, how could it do more?: "the very being of self-consciousness is such that in its being, its being is in question; this means that it is pure interiority. It is perpetually a reference to a *self* which it has to be" (*BN*, 241).

If the bonds of solidarity are built upon objectivity, then we must recall that subjectivity and objectivity are incommensurate modes of being. From the point of view of subjectivity, all objectivity involves distantiation. Thus with the appearance of one's own Look at the Other, solidarity collapses: "the *Us* collapses as soon as the for-itself reclaims its selfness in the face of the Third and looks at him in turn" (*BN*, 422). Placing the basis of social phenomena in the Looking-Looked-at dyad indicates that the *Us* is just as psychological as the *We*, and can be turned on and off almost at will.

In summary, in his "Presentation," Sartre's stress on social conditioning, liberation, and solidarity signals a change in his thought. He does not pause to relate these new themes to his earlier work, but it is clear that some revision is necessary in order to incorporate intelligibly these new themes. Their further elaboration would determine how radical a revision, if that is the appropriate word, would be called for.

SAINT GENET: ACTOR AND MARTYR

"Perhaps the book where I have best explained what I mean by freedom is, in fact, *Saint Genet*" (*BEM*, 35). The question is whether what freedom means in *Saint Genet* is the same as or compatible with freedom as it is worked out in *Being and Nothingness*. Mark Poster is representative of excellent critics and commentators on Sartre's works who see no disjuncture between *Saint Genet* and the early work represented by *Being and Nothingness*.

> *Saint Genet* developed the project of *Being and Nothingness*. . . . We can observe in *Saint Genet* Sartre's initial philosophical project growing, expanding, taking

new turns, and preserving its original impulses. There was no *coupure*, no break in the development of his thought, only a dialectic of growth, return and resynthesis, of statement, dispersal of interests and reunification.[1]

It is clear that in keeping faith with human freedom in *Saint Genet,* Sartre's project remained in principle intact. A case can be made, however, that *Saint Genet* did imply a transformative turn in his thought. Recall that Sartre had referred to *Being and Nothingness* as his "eidetic of bad faith" and that his concern was to understand this phenomenon, seek out its motive, and offer a cure. The difficulty is that *Saint Genet* does not neatly fit into this problematic. *Being and Nothingness* assumed that there were only two types of people, those in bad faith, attempting to flee their freedom, and those who were authentic, accepting and shouldering the burden of their freedom. The assumption of both attitudes was that everyone *knew* that he or she was free. One who would claim ignorance of freedom was guilty of bad faith. As Sartre unfolds the story of Jean Genet's life, beginning with his childhood, it is clear that Genet did not realize that he was free. For most of his life, Genet's self-conception did not include freedom, yet Sartre did not blame him for this. Rather he blames the "decent folk" who made Genet their "creature." If bad faith could be called a form of alienation inflicted upon oneself, Genet exemplifies a form of alienation inflicted upon one through the social conditioning Sartre had first discussed in his "Presentation."

What is especially striking in *Saint Genet* is the change of vocabulary to emphasize *passivity:* "the well-behaved child is *transformed* into a hoodlum"; Genet is "suddenly *provided* with a monstrous and guilty ego"; "he has been *provided* with a nature . . . a destiny." The very fact that Sartre would begin the story of "the making of Genet" with his childhood is itself remarkable. Children did not appear in *Being and Nothingness*. All talk of "origins" or "genetic" processes was "metaphysical" hypothesis. The for-itself, while temporal, was not portrayed in terms of stages of growth and development. Birth was not connected with the intelligibility of the for-itself's behavior. In *Saint Genet* the for-itself takes on a personal history that is essential to understanding social alienation and liberation.

The transformative moment in Genet's life, Sartre tells us, came when adults judged him to be a thief. The illegitimate Genet, an outsider from birth, comprehended that he had to possess things in order to be like the Other. When he appropriated things to himself, his action was judged a crime. In the eyes of others, Genet was a thief; he was given a nature. The child Genet believed this judgment. From that moment his life became "a matter of progressively internalizing the sentence imposed by adults" (*SG,* 47). This is a case of "alienation" being inflicted upon its victims:

This type of alienation is widespread. Most of the time, however, it is a matter of partial or temporary alienation. Now when children are subjected, from their earliest days, to great social pressure, when their Being-for-Others is the subject of a collective image accompanied by value judgments and social prohibitions, the alienation is sometimes total and definitive. This is the case of most pariahs in caste societies. They internalize the objective and external judgments which the collectivity passes on them, and they view themselves in their subjective individuality on the basis of an "ethnic character," a "nature," an "essence" which merely expresses the contempt in which *others* hold them. (*SG*, 44)

To those familiar with Sartre's early works, his claim that alienation can be "total and definitive" is surprising, even shocking. It smacks of an uncharacteristic fatalism and determinism. By calling this phenomenon "alienation," however, Sartre is not denying that Genet and pariahs are ontologically free. "Things" can not be alienated, only free beings. Nonetheless, as we have already indicated, the cases of Genet and pariahs do not fit into *Being and Nothingness,* although Sartre attempts to interpret their cases in terms of subjectivity and objectivity, the prevailing methodology of *Being and Nothingness.* For example, for the socially alienated there is "priority of the object over the subject, of what one is to others over what one is to oneself" (*SG*, 46). Again, in such instances, "We have given primacy to the object which we are to Others over the subject we are to ourself" (*SG*, 43). By taking the object over the subject, Genet is called a "wrong-way Descartes." Of course, by saying that "we have given" primacy to the object, Sartre does not mean "flight." He insists that Genet and pariahs are not at fault.

If we want to find the real culprits in this affair, let us turn to the decent folk and ask them by what strange cruelty they made of a child their scapegoat. (*SG*, 33)

But what happens, then, to the poor wretch on whom the decent man has projected all his evil desires, his sadism, his homicidal impulses and his lustful dreams? . . . He must incorporate these desires into himself, must internalize them, must make them *his* desires. (*SG*, 45)

Genet, and pariahs, do not flee from their freedom since they do not know they are free. The story of Genet's liberation is that of a human being coming gradually to discover his freedom. Genet comes to "recreate" this being which had been created by others. Sartre sketches out a type of logic to Genet's learning process and sees it as a process characteristic of all oppressed people. Genet must live his life on terms set by Others. Such a life is a repetition and confirmation of the initial judgment of Others. The oppressed come to view themselves with the eyes of Others. The initial choice can only be one of defiantly choosing and even flaunting their nature. Thus, Genet "decided to be what crime made of me." It was this "decision" that contained the seeds of his liberation. As Sartre points out, if one already *is*, there is no sense to a *project to be*. Genet's project to be a thief implied his lack of being and freedom. He attempted to confirm his being to Others by writing. Through the project of writing he became aware of his freedom, of his capacity to shape his being in the eyes of Others. The lesson Sartre finds in Genet's life, the understanding of freedom he derived from his study of Genet, is

> that in the end one is always responsible for what is made of one. Even if one can do nothing else besides assuming this responsibility. For I believe that a man always makes something out of what is made of him. This is the limit I would today accord to freedom, the small movement which makes of a totally conditioned social being someone who does not render back completely what his conditioning has given him. (*BEMIT*, 34–35)

While this victory for freedom is consistent with the commitment to freedom in Sartre's preceding works, the study of Genet poses serious problems in several ways for Sartre's ontology.

The first problem relates to the clarity with which the for-itself comprehended its freedom in *Being and Nothingness*. As noted in the last chapter, pre-reflective consciousness is not a pure immediacy. There is a "reflexivity" even on the pre-reflective level. By virtue of this self-awareness, the for-itself apprehends itself as other than its objects: "this nothingness is not anything except human reality apprehending itself as excluded from being and perpetually beyond being" (*BN*, 181). "I must necessarily possess a certain comprehension of freedom" (*BN*, 439). As Sartre put it in the *Cahiers:* "There is in all human activity a comprehension of the human condition and of freedom" (*C*, 488). In order to accommodate Genet, and the pariah, this self-comprehension (a progeny of Descartes's *cogito*) must be dimmed. Sartre remarked about Genet that because of social conditioning "the original intuition of his being is denied him" (*SG*, 55). Genet goes through a painful process in which he *learns* that he is free, in his case learning of his freedom through writing. The direct and immediate knowledge of freedom through "reflexivity" is displaced in terms of action.[2]

There is another aspect to the challenge that *Saint Genet: Actor and Martyr* poses to the earlier theory of consciousness. In depicting Genet's alienation, Sartre writes: "Here we have the key to Genet. That is what must be understood first: Genet is a child who has been convinced that he is, in his very depths, Another than Self" (*SG*, 45–46). Sartre uses the word "internalize" to portray how this Otherness enters the self. Since according to Sartre's ontology nothing alien can really enter into consciousness, he must claim that Genet only *believes* that something like a nature is *in* him. The practical effect of the belief is devastating, since Genet acts as if he had a nature. As we shall see, as Sartre continues to probe the notion of alienation—even his own in *The Words*—he will introduce an opaqueness into consciousness which has the effect of altering his previous view of consciousness in the direction of allowing otherness into the self.

Finally, the study of Genet introduces the concept of development into the discussion of consciousness, subjectivity, and self. In *Being and Nothingness* the for-itself, as we have noted, did not pass through any of the usual stages of life. The very notion of *self* appeared immediately, correlatively with that of the Other, or object. The study of Genet, by joining self to action and passion, reveals a concrete sense of self, an historical self. It is only by reference to a concrete, developing, historical self that Sartre can make sense of alienation and liberation, and in his subsequent works such a notion of self becomes paramount. The work on Flaubert, with its emphasis upon "the personalization of the individual," is, as we shall see, the culmination of Sartre's move in the direction of the concrete self.

The work of Wilfried Ver Eecke[3] and Mitchell Aboulafia[4] must be mentioned in connection with the development of consciousness in Sartre's work. They are specifically concerned with the relation between consciousness and negativity, and their work retains the spirit, if not the letter, of Sartre's own view of the relation between these notions. Each speaks of a constitution of subjectivity in terms of developmental psychology, with focus upon the infant and its relationship with others. Despite certain differences in detail, there is substantial agreement between the views of Ver Eecke and Aboulafia. Children learn, at a certain stage of experience and in certain circumstances, to say *no*. The appearance of this ability is coincidental with their sense of individuation. Prior to this, identification, of varying degrees, marked their lives. For Aboulafia, the child learns to say *no* by internalizing prohibitions given it by others. Only through the encouragement of others will the child be able to realize this ability, assume autonomy, and be capable of reciprocity. The Sartrean connection between negation, freedom, and individuality is preserved, but these phenomena are viewed as emerging in a developmental context. Ver Eecke and Aboulafia are sensitive to the crucial role of others in the development process and indicate how the realization of these phenomena can be stunted or aborted under certain conditions. In this way they stress the *mediation* necessary for a subjectivity to realize itself, and point out that conflict is not the *original* relationship with Others. Rather it can characterize a certain stage of development. *Saint Genet: Actor and Martyr* invites and is compatible with such developmental theories ("Since the child's objective essence was the NO, Genet gave himself a personality by giving himself the subjectivity of the NO," *SG*, 641). Sartre will offer his own version when he comes to study Flaubert.

The study of Genet, then, is an extended reflection on the force of circumstances, the power of social conditioning. It is clear that Genet does not fit into the categories of *Being and Nothingness*. In order to accommodate

Genet, these former theoretical categories must be either modified or now understood to reflect the structures of a developmental stage.

THE COMMUNISTS AND PEACE

The Communists and Peace, comprising several articles of Sartre which appeared in *Les Temps Modernes* from 1952 to 1954, was published in book form in 1964. "Topical" and "occasional" would suitably characterize these essays which, as Sartre tells us, were written "at top speed, with rage in my heart," provoked by political events of the time. The immediate provocation was the arrest by the French government of certain officials of the French Communist Party on the flimsiest evidence in order to prevent them from organizing mass protests. The Communist Party subsequently called for strikes in retaliation, and the workers only feebly responded. The main message Sartre hammers out is that the Communist Party is the only hope for unity and for galvanizing the proletariat to effective action, and that the workers, and other critics of the government, ought to recognize this. Sartre appears as angry at the non-Communist Left, epitomized by Claude Lefort,[5] as he is at the French Government. As in his "Presentation" he is contemptuous of a position he himself only recently enthusiastically embraced. He offers no excuses. No matter. Before long he will come to repudiate the position he is now taking.

Despite its occasional context, *The Communists and Peace* is an important text for our purposes. In significant ways it is a source for the major categories of the *Critique of Dialectical Reason* (series, counter-finality, group action), and is an intermediary text between *Saint Genet: Actor and Martyr* and the *Critique of Dialectical Reason.* While *Saint Genet: Actor and Martyr* focused upon social alienation, it showed little appreciation for social structures. Toward the very end of the book Sartre does acknowledge that genuine reciprocity "is concealed by the historical conditions of class and race, by nationalities, by the social hierarchy" (*SG,* 635). The thrust of the presentation of alienation, however, remains psychological, featuring the Look. *The Communists and Peace* continues Sartre's probing of *la force des choses* in terms of the class struggle. The early 1950s mark a serious political awakening for Sartre and, with the enthusiasm of the newly converted, he tends to become preachy about the class struggle. There remains a tendency to employ psychological categories even in making sense of the class struggle, but one can see a growing awareness of insight into the role of material conditions. One of the central issues for Sartre is the formation of class consciousness. This is a bone of contention between him and liberals such as Lefort. Sartre's view is that class consciousness is *made:* "Classes don't just happen to exist, they are made" (*CP,* 96). Class is not "the identity of items in a collection," and thus objectivities such as income, diet, health care, etc., do not constitute a class. In *Being and Nothingness* the role of the

Third was offered as the explanation for the *Us* and this was extended to the idea of class. While the Third will also play a pivotal role in formation of class in *The Communists and Peace,* the formation is more nuanced and is sensitive to mediations, for Sartre recognizes that "the system of production is for a class the necessary condition of its ability to exist" (*CP,* 89). Factors such as "the development of capital and the role of the worker in bourgeois society" evidence that the protelarist is not an "arbitrary" (or psychological) grouping of individuals, but he insists that these factors are not *sufficient* to form class consciousness. The potential for class is accounted for by the system of production. Those workers who suffer the effects of the system are characterized by passivity and alienation. Caught up within structures beyond their control, these "masses" are destined to live out their lives within these structures, "enclosed in the insipid world of repetition" (*CP,* 51).

The worker, no matter how far he goes back

> in the past, finds himself *already committed to and enlisted in* a society which has its code and its jurisprudence, its government, its notion of what is just and unjust, and (a more serious fact still) whose ideology he spontaneously shares. Society imposes on him a destiny, it systematically inflicts on him both fragmented and semi-automatic tasks, the sense and law of which escape him, and occupational disease. By fatigue and misery, by obliging him to reiterate the same gestures a thousand times a day, society discourages him from exercising his human qualities; . . . little by little he becomes a *thing.* (*CP,* 51)

Sartre's discovery of these social and economic structures leads him to accept the notion of *objective possibilities:* "The historical whole determines our powers at any given moment, it prescribes their limit in our field of action and our *real* future" (*CP,* 80). The plight of the masses is even more discouraging because of their isolation. They are "molecular scatterings, the mechanical aggregate of isolation, the pure product of the automation of tasks" (*CP,* 206). Sartre reiterates his disdain for the bourgeois analytic turn of mind and its emphasis upon abstract rights: "formal freedoms are chains." But Sartre now begins to see how in their isolation the masses injure themselves, as when they, by their efforts, compete against one another for jobs by being willing to work for the barest wages: "Then the social world is inhabited by actions which have lost their agents" (*CP,* 277). It is here that Sartre argues for the mediating function of the Communist Party: "Mediation is necessary between the working class, an activity as a historical enterprise, and the masses, the passive product of production. There must be *someone* to transform into upward thrust the weight which drags the masses down" (*CP,* 278). So lost in passivity is the worker of the masses that "he has been deprived of all initiative, since he has been stripped of his thought, how would he know that ideas are the products of men?" (*CP,* 193). What is called for in the masses is "an internal revolution" whereby the worker "will become *a different man* only by a sort of transformation. And he cannot have a presentiment of the sudden appearance of another universe and of another self as the subject of history so long as he remains crushed on his rock: how could passivity imagine activity?" (*CP*, 127). Through the mediation of the Communist Party the masses enter the class "by a synthetic act of unification which, by necessity, is distinguished from the mass as pure action is distinguished from passion" (*CP*, 129). The masses learn to say no: "The worker makes a proletarian of himself to the very extent that he refuses his state" (*CP*, 98). The worker becomes a subject by entering the proletariat and the Party is the necessary vehicle for the transformation, since it accounts for unity of will and action. It "deciphers" the befuddled consciousness of the masses and interprets it for them. There is salvation only in unity and, Sartre argues here, unity requires authority.

> The working class has coherence and power only insofar as it has confidence in its leaders. As for the authority of its leadership, I see also that it is neither usurped nor illusory. The leader interprets the situation, illuminates it by his plans, at his own risk, and the working class, by observing the directives, *legitimizes* the authority of the leader. . . . Today, a worker in France can express and fulfill himself only in a class action directed by the Communist Party. (*CP*, 272, 131)

The Communists and Peace evidences Sartre's deepening awareness of situatedness and continues the investigation of social alienation and solidarity. In the process, he also continues to create problems of continuity with the categories of his earlier thought. Readers of the early work would recognize the general characteristic of being for-itself in what Sartre portrays in *The Communists and Peace* as *praxis* or proletarian historical subjectivity. This is the subjectivity that surpasses the given toward its ends, a creative shaping of the future of its terms. But what Sartre refers to as "the masses," or with Marx as "sub-humanity," would be totally unfamiliar to these readers, as was Genet and the pariah. "The mass is *exteriority*" (*CP*, 95). The workers who constitute the masses are an "amalgam of necessity and autonomy" (*CP*, 125). The workers are free in that they use tools, choose among the objective possibilities offered by their field of action, etc., but they are not conscious of their freedom. They do not even know "that ideas are products of men." The masses are a curious admixture of the characteristics of being-for-itself and being-in-itself. As in the case of Genet, there is reference, to explain this alienation, to an element of alterity entering into consciousness: "in this subjectivity the interior is the pure interiorization of the exterior" (*CP*, 246). The consciousness of the masses is confused and incapable of critique, or of what Sartre referred to formerly as "purifying reflection." What Sartre said of the individual, Genet, is transposed to the existence and development of classes in *The Communists and Peace*. In both instances, however, a model of intelligibility is being developed which goes beyond that of the ontology of pure opposition of interior/exterior, self/other.

In addition to his growing awareness of the objective structures of the situation that contribute to understanding passivity, Sartre exhibits a firmer appreciation of solidarity. He tells us that class is "a *real* unity" (*CP*, 97) and "a new proximity of each to all" (*CP*, 89). Moreover, he now claims that it is only in fellowship with others that one is truly free: "it is by community of action and not in isolation that each would become a person" (*CP*, 94). He even offers a hypothesis of "identification" to account for this "real" unity: "I must perceive his situation and his needs as *my* situation and *my* needs in such a manner that his behavior appears to me *outside* like a project springing forth from my head; the imitator and imitated are at one and the same time interchangeable and separated, and imitative behavior is the result of a dialectic of identity and exteriority" (*CP*, 208). In his attempt to make intelligible the phenomenon of solidarity, Sartre is reaching toward a model which would allow him to express the unity that he now acknowledges as necessary. The notion of "dialectic" suggests itself as a way of bringing together interior and exterior, which had been frozen into opposition in the earlier work.

THE WORDS

Should someone unfamiliar with any of Sartre's other writings read *The Words*, or should it happen for some reason that only *The Words* was available to posterity, readers would never discover Sartre the philosopher of the power of consciousness. They would instead encounter a man with an almost fatalistic assessment of the human condition. From the early genealogy (Louis begot Albert, Charles begot Anna Marie . . .) to the self-doubts of the conclusion, the power of lucid self-creation has been displaced. "Were it not for that mistake," Sartre interjected, in referring to an incident in his life, "I would now be a monk" (*W*, 61).

The Words was published in 1964, but Sartre tells us that the greater part of it was written in 1954, the time immediately following *Saint Genet* and *The Communists and Peace*, the time during which he came to believe in the class struggle and political commitment. He was then an angry man, and *The Words* seems to be a confessional response to the fact that he indeed had taken positions—such as the aesthetic solution to life—that he was now violently condemning. Sartre had discovered that all along he was a bourgeois. With a sense of embarrassment he recognizes his "bourgeois, puritan individualism" (*W*, 91). As the decent folk had made a monster of Genet, so he himself now claims had been made a monster by adults: "I was a child, that monster which they had fabricated" (*W*, 52). This making of Sartre is the theme of his brief autobiography, which extends only to his pre-teen years.

Sartre informs his readers that, given his particular life-situation—his father's early death, his mother's return with the infant Sartre to her parent's home, the adulation of the family group for the young Sartre, his grandfather's deep love of books—he turned out to be the kind of person he is. Specifically, his family gave him the impression that his existence was of intrinsic worth. Upon entering school, he discovered that he was an ugly little shrimp in whom his peers were not interested; in order to secure his necessity and worth, he retreated into the life of imagination, reading and writing. His "neurosis" was his way of protecting himself from contingency.

He is particularly repentant about *Nausea*. While it is clear from interviews that he continued to hold the literary quality of his novel in high regard, he rejects its notion of salvation.

> Choice had made me a man, generosity would make me a book. I could cast my missive, my mind, in letters of bronze; I could replace the rumblings of my life by irreplaceable inscriptions, my flesh by a style, the faint spirals of time by eternity. (*W*, 121)

> At the age of thirty, I executed the masterstroke of writing in *Nausea*—quite sincerely, believe me—about the bitter unjustified existence of my fellowmen and of exonerating my own. . . . Fake to the marrow of my bones and hoodwinked, I joyfully wrote about our unhappy state. (*W*, 157–58)

In claiming that he had been "hoodwinked" Sartre is acknowledging the passivity of his conditioning: "I had not *chosen* my vocation; it had been imposed on me by others" (*W*, 129). "External forces shaped my flight and made me" (*W*, 156). To account for this conditioning, he continues the language adopted since *Saint Genet: Actor and Martyr,* to the effect that alterity enters the self: "The grownups . . . were installed in my soul" (*W*, 129) and "a tremendous collective power had entered me" (*W*, 157).

It is true that Sartre is writing *The Words* with the perspective of a reflective analysis, and from within this perspective he declares, "I have changed." He appears to have cleansed himself: "I collared the Holy Ghost in the cellar and threw him out. . . . I've lost my illusions" (*W*, 158). This appears a triumph for the power of consciousness after all. Yet, significantly, Sartre hesitates and in effect casts his cure into ambiguity. This

> recently acquired knowledge undermines my old certainties without quite destroying them. (*W*, 156)

> Moreover, that old crumbling structure, my imposture, is also my character: one gets rid of a neurosis, one doesn't get cured of one's self. Though they are worn out, blurred, humiliated, thrust aside, ignored, all of the child's traits are still to be found in the quinquagenarian. Most of the time they lie low, they bide

their time; at the first moment of inattention, they rise up and emerge, disguised; I claim sincerely to be writing for my time, but my present notoriety annoys me; it's not glory since I'm alive, and yet that's enough to belie my old dreams; could it be that I still harbor them secretly? (*W*, 189)

This hesitation and ambiguity challenge, on a concrete level, the power of consciousness. First of all, social conditioning, as we have observed, is discussed in terms of alterity entering the self. In the passage just referred to this is exemplified when Sartre writes that "all of the child's traits are still to be found in the quinquagenarian." Secondly, the possibility of effecting a purifying or cleansing reflection, which affords critique and allows liberation, is put in question. *The Words* ends with a suspiciousness about reflective knowledge and action: "could it be that I still harbor them secretly?" In *Saint Genet: Actor and Martyr* and *The Communists and Peace*, the result of social conditioning was often presented as a passivity and ineffectuality, while there always appeared its opposite number, a life of rehabilitated subjectivity, *praxis*, pure reciprocity. With *The Words* Sartre is introducing a certain scepticism about authenticity as a pure type of existence, one itself free of alterity. Reflection or knowledge as such does not have the power to allow one to start from scratch. This is what Sartre meant when in an interview entitled "On *The Idiot of the Family*" the interviewer raised the question of the discovery of Sartre's own neurosis and the possibility of self-analysis. Sartre responds by talking about the experience of re-reading himself. He discovers aspects of himself of which he was previously unaware and admits that "if I try to study myself, assumptions will inevitably enter the picture because of my loyalty, or my adherence, to myself" (*IF-L/ S*, 121). Then the interviewer asked: "When you say this aren't you saying that what you called pure or nonaccessory reflection in *Being and Nothingness*—which is a requirement for authenticity—is impossible?" Sartre replied:

> You know that I never described this kind of reflection; I said it could exist, but I only showed examples of accessory reflection. And later I discovered that non-accessory reflection was not different from the accessory and immediate way of looking at things but was the critical work one can do on oneself during one's entire life, through *praxis*. (*IF-L/S*, 132)

Another clear bifurcation of the early work, that between inauthentic and authentic existence, is undermined under the pressure of thinking through *la force des choses*. Our past, our character, have come to have a *weight* they did not have under the thesis of the power of consciousness. The closer Sartre comes to the concrete, the more his former dualisms lose their explanatory power. Human reality appears progressively to be an "amalgam" of necessity/autonomy, activity/passivity, subjectivity/objectivity, clarity/obscurity, self/other.

Hazel Barnes, in assessing the period we have been discussing, the time of the discovery of *la force des choses* culminating in *The Words*, writes: "For us who observe from the outside, Sartre's shift in attitude in the mid-fifties seems less of a watershed than it appeared to him. Outwardly the effect on his career was far less striking than the decision he arrived at in the year 1940 when for the first time he recognized the obligation to prove himself politically."[6] The shift as we have been discussing it is not simply one from thought to action but one which involves a new understanding of consciousness, situation, freedom, Others. In this sense it does mark a watershed for Sartre's philosophy. Unfortunately, at the time he did not pause to reconsider his earlier work (except in the case of *Nausea*) in the light of his newly emerging thinking, outside of general remarks to the effect that some of the language he had used to describe freedom "strikes me as absurd today" and that while "There's no question that there is some basic change in the concept of freedom, I still remain faithful to the notion of freedom" (*SBH*, 58). Perhaps the closest he comes to admitting an important, detailed modification of his early work is his new view of "experience" which we will soon examine: "The conception of 'lived experience' marks my change since *L'Être et Le Néant*" (*BEMIT*, 41). This new conception allows for "opaqueness," "blindness," "absence" in consciousness and is not fully translatable into concepts. As we have noted some time previously, this change compels Sartre to declare that subjectivity and objectivity are "entirely useless notions" to him. Yet the whole enterprise of his ontology in *Being and Nothingness* and his defense of the free project was based upon the subject/object, self/Other distinctions. How could he modify his view of experience in such a way without serious fallout for his earlier categories?

In addition to the change of views about experience to allow for alterity in consciousness, Sartre experiences changes in his view of social relationships. Under the impact of *la force des choses,* he tells an interviewer:

Our lives inside and outside, subjective and objective, personal and political—all necessarily awake echoes in one another because they are aspects of one and the same whole, and one can understand an individual, whoever he may be, by seeing him as a social being. (*SP-L/S*, 44)

I abandoned my pre-war individualism and the idea of the pure individual and adopted the social individual and socialism. That was the turning point of my life: before and after. (*SP-L/S*, 48)

There is no denying that Sartre has come to recognize the reality of solidarity and class, but his treatment of human sociality takes off in two different directions that will require reconciliation. On the one hand, in discussing class, he employs the model of building wholes out of units. His starting point is isolated individuals, who through an outside stimulus, the Third, are brought into a form of unity and thereby modified in a significant manner. The nature of this unity in its relationship to the individuals which comprise it is referred to as an "autonomy" and left unprobed. On the other hand, in *Saint Genet: Actor and Martyr* and *The Words*, where child development is stressed, the notion of the isolated individual is differently considered. Strictly speaking, from birth, the socialization process begins. One can survive and grow only in relationship with Others, and from the start these relationships are formative of the self. Individualization is a possible stage in the on-going developmental process. From this perspective, human beings do not become social; they are in continuous stages of socialization. The first dimension of sociality might be called the Marxist problematic since it deals with human relationships mediated by productive forces, and the second Freudian, since it deals with infancy, childhood, and family relationships. Sartre had hoped to combine these explanatory models in *Saint Genet: Actor and Martyr,* but he recognized that he had failed, since his undertanding of productive forces was so poor at that time. He would try again in his study of Flaubert, with the tools he fashioned in *Critique of Dialectical Reason.*

We have observed the impact upon Sartre of *la force des choses* and its translation into the recognition of social alienation and solidarity. We will now turn to consider the theoretical works in which Sartre attempted to forge new categories to illuminate these newly revealed phenomena. Then, since Sartre has not explicitly reviewed his earlier categories, we will have to assess not only the power of his new categories to illuminate phenomena but also the relationship between earlier and later categories.

FOUR

Mediations

*Search for a Method, Critique of Dialectical Reason*I, and *The Family Idiot* are studies rich in interest in a number of ways and, indeed, many fine works of commentary and critique have explored various of the perspectives opened up by these works. Our approach to these texts will be circumscribed by their relevance to our dual themes of social conditioning and solidarity. Each of these works can be seen to forge categories appropriate to making these phenomena intelligible.

SEARCH FOR A METHOD

Phenomenology was the method Sartre adopted in order to approach concrete experience, and he claimed to always have remained a phenomenologist. Yet it is apparent in the articles written at the close of the fifties and published as *Search for a Method* that phenomenology is inadequate by itself to cope with the new "concrete" experience of social conditioning. Each of the pieces that comprise *Search for a Method* repeats in one form or other Marx's assertion that human beings are both producers and products. He accepts "without reservation" Engels's contention that "men themselves make their history but in a given environment which conditions them." Throughout *Search for a Method* there is an attempt to articulate the sense of "conditions" in the Engels statement. Phenomenology was a model that, under Sartre's hermeneutics, provided an existentialist theory of "production" and freedom, but it failed to reveal the extent to which subjects are themselves constituted. The subject/object bifurcation and the ontology of negation were used to separate the self from any imposition of foreign meaning or conditioning. The existentialist self which emerged from Sartre's appropriation of phenomenology was defined in terms of activity, not passivity: "Indeed by the sole fact that I am conscious of the causes which inspire my action, these causes are already transcendent objects for my consciousness, they are totally outside it" (*BN*, 439). "It is impossible for objects to act upon consciousness" (*BN*, 442). "Being in the world is a choice . . . this choice is always unconditioned" (*BN*, 457, 479).

Sartre's growing sensitivity to social conditioning leads him to employ language which shows this. He speaks repeatedly of the intrusion of otherness. Moreover, there is growing recognition of influences that alienate self and action, which are not thematic and which operate as it were behind one's back so as to be outside the subject/object model of experience. In *Search for a Method* Sartre develops a new methodology in which phenomenology will factor as a "phase of phenomenological description" to be complemented and completed by regressive and progressive investigations.

The rethinking of methodology begins with some general, sketchy, but nonetheless startling comments on philosophy itself. Philosophy is, Sartre states matter-of-factly, *praxis:* "every philosophy is practical" (*SM*, 5), radically situated in a social context and defined by the needs and tensions of its context. The idea of a perennial philosophy is ridiculed. The investigator is always implicated in the investigation. Philosophy is a totalization, a synthetic labor of thought, but always itself exists within a number of on-going totalizations that comprise History itself. He appears to accept, and *Critique of Dialectical Reason* I will confirm, that the concepts used to understand *praxis* are "heuristic" and its "universals" contextual.

> But it is precisely a matter of testing, criticizing and establishing, *within History* and at this particular moment in the development of human societies, the instruments of thought by means of which History thinks itself insofar as they are also the practical instruments by means of which it is made. (*CDR* I, 40)

> Thus the universals of the dialectic—principles and laws of intelligibility—are individualized universals; attempts at abstraction and universalization can only result in schemata which are continually valid *for that process*. (*CDR* I, 49)

This general call to integrate theory and practice is bound to raise questions in the reader's mind about Sartre's previous work, particularly *Being and Nothingness,* which claimed "eidetic" certainty. But in *Search for a Method* Sartre is clearly on the move, too preoccupied with the present to revise past categories, if they do need revision. He does admit, in general, that existentialism was an historical moment (of bourgeois origin) in the ongoing totalization of thought. He is somewhat derogatory of existentialism, calling it an "enclave inside Marxism," and will later recant this, but the basic ontological truths of *Being and Nothingness* appear to remain, valid, in the background. From time to time, although fleetingly, for-itself, in-itself, and for-Others, make appearances in *Search for a Method, Critique of Dialectical Reason* and *The Family Idiot.* He plays off an apparent contradiction between existentialism (Kierkegaard) and history (Hegel), and proposes that both contain truths that can only be integrated in the thought of Marx. It is Marx's discourse which bears upon "the concrete," and in relation to which Kierkegaard and Hegel are abstractions. This move to a new notion of the concrete ("the concrete is history and dialectical action," *SM*, 20–21), signals a redefinition of the human being and freedom. "Concrete man" is "that man who is defined simultaneously by his needs, by the material condition of his existence, and by the nature of his work—that is, by his struggle against things and against men" (*SM*, 14). Concrete freedom is a freedom of objective possibilities. No longer is the situation simply "there" as the factual background for the projection of our possibilities, but is "a field of possibilities . . . a strongly structured region which depends upon all of History . . . on the social, historical reality" (*SM*, 93).

The notion of materiality is common to concrete human reality and freedom. "The material conditions of his existence circumscribe the field of his possibility," so that "the most individual possible is only the internalization and enrichment of a social possible" (*BN*, 93, 95). Throughout *Search for a Method* and *Critique of Dialectical Reason* are found not simply pairs, such as *praxis* and practico-inert, and their dialectical interrelatedness, but a bonding of these pairs in materiality in a way not present in *Being and Nothingness*. *Praxis* is the activity of the organism: *"praxis*, in the first instance, is nothing but the relation of the organism, as exterior and future end, to the present organism as a totality under threat" (*CDR* I, 83). In this view the organism is both active and passive. It appears that some modification to the categories of *Being and Nothingness* is in order.

While a thread of monistic, materialistic discourse wends its way throughout *Search for a Method* and *Critique of Dialectical Reason* I, it is clear that Sartre insists upon making room for freedom in his vision of social reality and history. The purpose of his investigation, he tells us, is to recover man's "veritable humanity—that is, the power to make History by pursuing his own ends" (*SM*, 164). Men are not "merely the vehicles of inhuman forces which through them would govern this social world" (*SM*, 87). Alienated human beings are not things, nor does alienation consist of "the physical laws governing external conditions" (*SM*, 91). Idealist Marxists cannot explain away the power of consciousness without absurd consequences for their own credibility. While the power of consciousness is present in *Search for a Method*, as well as *Critique of Dialectical Reason* I and *The Family Idiot*, Sartre's task will be to frame it in a discourse that will also make room for its profound alienations. He has no doubt that the appropriate discourse is that of *dialectic*. "We cannot conceive of this conditioning in any form except that of a dialectual movement": (*SM*, 34).

The implications of the move to a dialectical model are available by attending to the way that Sartre now looks at the *project*, which, as we have observed, is the central expression of the theory of the power of consciousness. He now tells us that "subjectivity is neither everything or nothing; it represents a moment in the objective process (that in which externality is internalized)" (*SM*, 33). The project is identified as this subjective moment: it is "the subjective surpassing of objectivity toward objectivity" (*SM*, 97). The project, while now becoming a moment in a process, nonetheless still retains the utmost significance, since it alone "can account for history" (*SM*, 99). It functions as a rejection of the view that "history" is a mechanical sequence of events. The project's role, however, is not simply described as a creation, or an unjustified, unconditional choice of being. It is "mediation": "the subjective contains within itself the objective, which it denies and which it surpasses toward a new objectivity" (*SM*, 98). The language, still that of subject/object, strains to express in a tortuous way an insight not congenial to the terms. The crucial language here is the expression "contains within itself" and the term "denies." The thrust of the language is not consonant with *Being and Nothingness*, where negation was equivalent to rupture, fission, break. Here the language allows for conservation. The project in both *Being and Nothingness* and *Search for a Method* is an instance of "surpassing the given," yet the intelligibility is different in early and later text. In *Search for a Method* "To surpass . . . is also to preserve" (*SM*, 10) and "the project retains and unveils the surpassed reality" (*SM*, 92). In the earlier texts, negation was depicted as rejection. In *The Transcendence of the Ego*, for example, Sartre claimed that "each moment of conscious life is a creation *ex nihilo.*" That the two notions of surpassing are conceptually different is evident in the phenomena of "coloration" and "spirals."

The project, Sartre tells us, "must cut across the field of instrumental possibilities" (*SM*, 111). When actions enter into this highly structured field and encounter the actions of others, "the consequences of our acts always end up escaping us, since every concerted enterprise, as soon as it is realized, enters into relation with the entire universe, and since this *infinite* multiplicity of relations goes beyond our intention" (*SM*, 47). The free project, in this process which will be fully delineated in *Critique of Dialectical Reason* I, can become twisted in such a way that it strikes back, with unintended results, at the agent. This is a significant way in which free projects become alienated. But there is another way: "the given, which we surpass at every instant by the simple fact of living it, is not restricted to the material condition of our existence; we must include in it . . . our own childhood" (*SM*, 100). In *Search for a Method*, social conditioning assumes two important dimensions. One is, broadly speaking, "Marxist," and accounts for the process by which *praxis* is deformed in such a way that the result of its actions is turned against it. The other is "Freudian" and accounts for the shaping of sense of self and character. In each case of alienation the project, as internalization of the external, takes on "traces" which define it.

> What was once both a vague comprehension of our class, of our social conditioning by way of the family group, and a blind going-beyond, an awkward effort to wrench ourselves away from all this, at last ends up inscribed in us in the form of *character.* At this level are found the learned gestures (bourgeois gestures, socialist gestures) and the contradictory roles which compose us and which tear us apart (e.g., for Flaubert, the role of the dreamy, pious child, and

that of future surgeon, the son of an atheistic surgeon). At this level also are the traces left by our first revolts, our desperate attempts to go beyond a stifling reality, and the resulting deviation and distortions. To surpass all that is also to preserve it. We shall think *with* these gestures which we have learned and which we want to reject. (*SM*, 101)

To "think with," to "act with," is a description of intentional activity itself. The intentional act comes to have a certain *coloration* by virtue of internalizing this external: "the gestures and roles are *inseparable* from the project which transforms them. . . . Surpassed and maintained, they constitute what I shall call the *internal coloration* of the project" (*SM*, 105; emphasis added). This notion of coloration is significant. In *Being and Nothingness*, the language in which the surpassing of the given is depicted is that of a sharp severence: "If the given can not explain the intention, it is necessary that the intention by its upsurge realize a rupture with the given. . . . It would be in vain to imagine that consciousness can exist without a given. . . . But if consciousness exists in terms of the given, this does not mean that the given conditions consciousness; consciousness is a pure and simple negation of this given" (*BN*, 478). When Sartre speaks in *Being and Nothingness* of interiorizing techniques, he emphasizes that the technique disappears into the free project, apparently losing its particular weight. The for-itself surpasses the technique toward its end, but in this interiorization it "loses its character as a technique and is interpreted purely and simply in the free surpassing of the given toward ends" (*BN*, 523). The tendency in *Being and Nothingness* is to separate clearly the pure project as negation of all exteriority from the objectification which it takes on only in the eyes of Others. Dialect, nationality, character traits, are, for subjectivity, only unrealizables. Their reality is in the eyes of Others. Subjective and objective are incommensurable. The notion of coloration shows that Sartre's dialectic of internal and external breaks down the separation of internal and external in *Being and Nothingness*. Likewise, in *Critique of Dialectical Reason* I, by shifting to the discourse of the organism, it is clear that the organism, in acting on the material world, is itself subject to the action of material effects which profoundly modify it. As will be seen, using a technique, such as a tool or a machine, in *Critique of Dialectical Reason* I involves an internalization that is profoundly influenced by these techniques.

The revised conception of surpassing the given in the new dialectical model leads Sartre to consider a human life as a *spiral:*

> Surpassing is not an instantaneous movement, it is a long work; each moment of this work is at once the surpassing and, to the extent that it is posited for itself, the pure and simple subsistence of these deviations at a given level of integration. For this reason a life develops in spirals; it passes again and again by the same points but at different levels of integration and complexity. (*SM*, 106)

A language of "development" and "integration" is now thought appropriate, in the context of dialectic, to represent human action. We will observe Sartre employing this model in his study of Flaubert, but for the present it is significant to note how both coloration and spiral, while not dwelt upon at any length, are evidence that the dialectical method turns away from the sharp dichotomies of *Being and Nothingness*. One of these sharp dichotomies, it is important to note, is the ontological understanding of temporality as "break in being," specifically the discourse relating, or unrelating, past and present as "absolute distance" wherein the past falls "out of my reach, without contact, without connections" (*BN*, 118). The temporality of totalization, characterized by traces and coloration, is hermeneutic in nature, with the image of the "spiral" replacing that of creation *ex nihilo*.

The closest Sartre comes to discussing solidarity and social reality is a brief reference to "collectives." By collectives here Sartre means groups such as family, neighborhood, workplace, religious affiliation, etc. His judgment is that Marxism "remains uncertain as to the nature and origin" of collectives. There is a strong tendency in Marxism to fall into an abstract thinking that fails to recognize "the reality of alienated individuals" and instead attempts to explain behavior by a direct relationship to mode of production. Marxism has not been sensitive to "mediation"—"the direct relations between persons depend upon other particular relations, and then on still others, and so on in succession" (*SM*, 78). Mediations allow for "the multi-dimensional *unity* of the act" (*SM*, 111) and "a relative autonomy" of levels of group experience. To affirm the "specificity" of an event is to take into account the various transactions between individuals and their environments. Dialectical social thought "must first be made to pass through a process of mediation, one which will bring into play the concrete men who were involved in it, the specific character it took on from its basic conditioning, the ideological instruments it employed" (*SM*, 42). An event in its concreteness "has its opaqueness which does not allow us to dissolve it in fundamental determinations" (*SM*, 79). It has its ambiguity: "a single act can be evaluated at more and more complex levels and consequently it is expressed by a series of very diverse significations" (*SM*, 108). While in this context Sartre does not use the concepts of coloration and spiral that he employs in talking about a single life, the entire discussion of conditioning does have its unity of intelligibility in the notion of *totalization*. I would argue that it is this notion which is the centerpiece of the dialectic, as project was of phenomenology. Totalization is not as prominently featured in *Search for a Method* as it will be in *Critique of Dialectical Reason* I and especially in *The Family Idiot*. Totalization is the very activity of *praxis*, a synthesizing of diversity in terms of an end. But since the life of *praxis* is a continual totalization, various levels of experience are continually being dialectically adjusted to one another as new experiences continue. Totalization is the dialectical movement of *praxis,* of internalizing and externalizing, of conserving and surpassing. In this sense it is the intelligible basis for all social conditioning, and, as the centerpiece of the dialectic, will have to be compared in the end with the ontological categories of *Being and Nothingness.*

The epistemological foundation of dialectical understanding is, Sartre tells us, "comprehension":

> To grasp the meaning of any human conduct it is necessary to have at our disposal what German psychiatrists and historians have called "comprehension." But what is involved here is neither a particular talent nor a special faculty of intuition; this knowing is simply the dialectical movement which explains the act by its terminal signification in terms of its starting conditions. (*SM,* 153)

Comprehension is a *savoir,* but not of the conceptual order. Commentators who have pointed out the roots of comprehension in Sartre's own theory of the non-positional self-consciousness are correct, but Sartre's reference to the German social science tradition here is noteworthy, for comprehension takes on a social dimension lacking in the Cartesian background of the non-positional self-consciousness. Comprehension is a participant's grasp of a shared situation.

> If my companion suddenly starts toward the window, I understand his gesture in terms of the material situation in which we both are. It is, for example, because the room is too warm. . . . In every way, if I am able to go beyond the succession of gestures and to perceive the unity which they give themselves, I must myself feel the overheated atmosphere as a need for freshness, as a demand for air; that is, I must myself become the lived surpassing our material situation. (*SM,* 153)

The key phrase in this text is "I understand his gesture in terms of the material situation in which we both are." As a project aware of itself, I understand from lived experience what it is to engage in intentional behavior. Although Sartre does not express it in this way, this forms a fundamental "prejudice" when I come to understand. When I encounter Others I grasp their activity in terms of intentionality. In this case, my anthropomorphic prejudice is just the key I need to understand their behavior. An encounter with people in a strange culture, however, might from the start be intelligible only in the limited way that would be able to recognize that these people are "doing something" and I would be led to interpret from my own experience as best I can what is they are doing. This very abstract grasp of their *praxis* must be differentiated from what is available to participants in a shared situation. To the latter the import of a gesture or act is immediately grasped across the shared practices of a common life-world. This is the sense of his remark in *Critique of Dialectical Reason* I that there is "limitation in the power of comprehension . . . due to the *position of the observer*" (*CDR* I, 696). Whether in abstract or in concrete form, comprehension includes regressive and progressive moments. The act is intelligible in terms of the end it aims at as well as of the conditions out of which it arises. Sartre insists that all conceptual knowledge of human beings "founds" itself "upon indirect, comprehensive knowledge" (*SM*, 174). All conceptual knowledge of human action must allow for the irreducibility of comprehension, that is, the nature of the intentional act itself. A person who intentionally acts to achieve a goal may do so in a mystified way or as alienated. Nonetheless, the act is intentional and all explanation of mystification and alienation must take that into account. "Human existence and the comprehension of the human are inseparable" (*SM*, 176).

By itself comprehension is unable to account for all social or historical phenomena. Since *praxis* inscribes itself in the universe and thereby into all the relationships of the universe, the intentional act is susceptible to non-intended consequences. These "acts with no authors" require an "intellection" which would incorporate analytic contributions from various disciplines appropriate for grasping objective structures. But in the end, this analytic contribution must be grasped in terms of its human genesis and be used for purposes of human control of life.

Search for a Method marks a change of method and tone. Dialectical intelligibility centers on the "between" of terms, upon interaction and mutual influence. Sartre is led to speak of relations as real, "real relations between men" (*SM*, 77). To accommodate the interactions, he is led toward an undefined monistic materialism. Internalization of the external "colors" the subjective project, employing a theory of negation as conserving. Totalizations integrate while preserving, allowing for plurality of meaning. Comprehension as a social epistemological tool replaces the subject/object, alienating grasp of Others in *Being and Nothingness*. Without developing these notions at length, *Search for a Method* gives every indication that, in response to the experience of the intrusion of otherness, Sartre's thinking is undergoing drastic revisions, reaching even into its fundamental categories.

CRITIQUE OF DIALECTICAL REASON I

Sartre continues his pursuit of the concrete, this time identified as "the absolute concrete historical man" (*CDR* I, 52). The concrete now is viewed as consisting of a multiplicity of totalizations enveloping and influencing one another. In the midst of on-going totalizations, where is one to begin an investigation? Specifically, how does the investigator, implicated in totalization, whose very effort to understand is itself a totalization, begin? Any beginning will be an abstraction, a thread focused upon, which will lead to other threads, which in turn will lead back to the initial thread, bringing thereby a transformation of the original understanding of that thread. For Sartre the initial thread is "the individual fulfilling himself in his abstract *praxis*" (*CDR* I, 52). Comprehension of *praxis* implicates regressive and progressive moments of intelligibility. In this first volume of *Critique of Dialectical Reason* Sartre chooses to pursue the regressive or, in general, those conditions on the basis of which men make history. Sartre is emphatic that he is not thereby offering an actual reading of history. Instead his intention is to provide, on a formal level ("this is a matter of *formal* intelligibility," (*CDR* I, 68), concepts and categories that enable a grasp of social conditioning ("the static condition of the possibility of a totalization," (*CDR* I, 68) useful down the line for a progressive account of history. What Sartre does is fashion, as an intelligible tool, a story which begins with an individual fulfilling himself or herself; this simple intention implicates ever more complicated relationships with the environment and with others, which, in turn, reverberate with alienating impact upon the agent. The story is a grim one, a desperate, relentless struggle to survive. A ray of hope emerges with the appearance of a concrete freedom in the group-in-fusion. But, all in all, it is a paralyzingly painful view of human existence. Our interest in the story is its relevance to social conditioning and solidarity. With regard to social conditioning our attention will center on Sartre's treatment of class, while our interest in solidarity will focus upon seriality and groups.

CLASS.

Class consists of "the *social Being* of man at the fundamental level, that is to say, insofar as there are *several people* within a practical field totalized by the mode of production" (*CDR* I, 230). While Sartre is indeed insisting on the connection between mode of production and class, he is not interested in providing a genetic account of class in the usual Marxist manner. His interest bears upon class as a particular type of structural existence.

Class does not have a reality of its own independent of its participants. Class as a structural mode of existence is a practico-inert phenomenon. *Praxis* as labor inscribes itself in matter, altering it, fixing it with a meaning it does not have in itself. This worked matter then exerts an exigency over *praxis*. When Sartre refers to class, he invariably means the proletariat talked about by Marx, those who are defined by means of production in the modern industrialized West, a means they do not own. To survive, the proletariat employs means that in turn define their lives: "individuals find an existence already sketched out for them at birth; they 'have their position in life' and their personal development assigned to them by their class" (*CDR* I, 232). Class being, in this sense, is passivity. He borrows a graphic depiction of an individual who suffers class being.

A working woman who earns 25,000 francs a month and contracts chronic eczema by handling Dop shampoo eight hours a day is wholly reduced to her work, her fatigue, her wages and the material impossibilities that these wages assign her: the impossibility of eating properly, of buying shoes, of sending her child to the country, and of satisfying her most moderate wishes. Oppression does not reach the oppressed in a particular sector of their life; it constitutes this life in totality. They are not people plus needs: they are completely reducible to their needs. There is no distance between self and self, no essence is hidden within the bounds of interiority: the person exists outside, in his relation to the world, and visible to all; he coincides exactly with his objective reality. (*CDR* I, 232)

One thinks of the example Sartre uses of the young woman at the end of *The Transcendence of the Ego*. As she waited for her husband to return from work, and was gazing at the passersby, she experienced, in terrifying anxiety, an indetermination with respect to her life. She was experiencing the present as a creation *ex nihilo*, or, in terms of *Being and Nothingness*, the radical break in being or distance from one's situation. This early example does not at all recognize the passivity of the woman in the shampoo factory. As if with this earlier example on his mind, Sartre asks,

Do we also have to admit that one is a worker *passively?* Existentialism denied the *a priori* existence of essences; must we not now admit that they do exist and that they are the *a priori* characteristics of our passive being? And if they exist, how is *praxis* possible? I used to say that one never *is* a coward or a thief. Accordingly, should I not now say that one *makes oneself* a bourgeois or a proletarian? (*CDR* I, 231)

Sartre replies to his own question that indeed one makes oneself proletarian or bourgeois, but "in order to make oneself bourgeois, one must be bourgeois" (*CDR* I, 231). He rejects the comparison between a characteristic such as cowardice, which is only a characteristic in the eyes of the Other and is not subjective, and "membership in a class." What, then, does Sartre mean by *being* a proletarian or bourgeois? He goes on to explain the meaning of this being as a transcendence-transcended.

The worker is a transcendence. The worker uses tools, language, makes choices about budgeting money, etc. The woman in the shampoo factory decides to abort rather than raise a child in poverty: "class-being does not prevent us from realising an individual destiny" (*CDR* I, 239). In this sense "existential principles are unaffected" (*CDR* I, 235). In the context of social alienation, however, "*transcending one's class condition* effectively means realizing it" (*CDR* I, 238). Because workers are "located, in spite of themselves, inside a framework of references that cannot be transcended, they simply realize everyone's class being. Everyone makes himself signify by interiorizing, by a free choice, the signification with which material exigencies have produced him as a *significant being" (CDR* I, 238). The exigencies act like an essence since, within their influence, actions are equivalent to repetition. Even the type of fantasies imagined by workers of semi-automatic machines is a realization of their objective condition: "the deepest interiority becomes a means of realizing oneself as total exteriority" (*CDR* I, 234). The very humanistic rebellion of workers in the nineteenth century against their being exploited, which incorporated their being divided into skilled and unskilled workers, expressed the prevailing material conditions: "the organization against exploitation recreated, rigorously but freely, all the conditions which materiality imposes on alienated man" (*CDR* I, 243). Material conditions, while not related to human action as cause to effect, dialectically constrain action. They can, in fact, perform something like a coloration of action: "Indeed it can always be said that any material circumstance which has to be transcended, even the configuration of the land in the course of a walk, imposes a certain content on the future towards which it is transcended" (*CDR* I, 235). Thus, once more, "surpassing the given" is seen to be a form of conservation.

The alienations so far discussed with respect to class have featured the process through which a free action, inscribing itself in matter, becomes diverted into an exigency which defines the agent. *Critique of Dialectical Reason* I is replete with excellent examples of such "counter finality." There is, however, another form of alienation, perhaps more insidious, which is referred to just prior to the discussion of class and which can be easily applied to class. The alienation in question, an "alienation of knowledge," strikes at the agent's sense of self. The sentence that precedes the treatment of class reads: "All of us spend our lives engraving our maleficent image on things, and it fascinates and bewilders us if we try to understand ourselves *through it,* although we are ourselves the totalizing movement which results in *this* particular objectification" (*CDR* I, 227). Ths issue named as the "alienation of knowledge" has its roots in the study of Genet and will be taken up in detail in the study of Flaubert. Recall that the problem as it arose in the Genet study regarded Genet's self-conception. As a wrong-way Descartes, Genet obtained his sense of self from Others rather than through his self-consciousness. We noted that Genet was not guilty of bad faith in the sense of *Being and Nothingness,* for Genet was not fleeing from a freedom he would not accept. Others hid Genet's freedom from him. The dominating role of self-consciousness in *Being and Nothingness* was displaced in order to account for Genet and the pariah. Now, in *Critique of Dialectical Reason* I, Sartre addresses this displacement as an alienation of knowledge. By inscribing oneself in external form, one thinks of oneself in inert terms. Sartre now claims that initially the free agent knows himself or herself through that inert form. Heidegger, of course, whose understanding of being-in-the-world is such that Dasein can only grasp itself through the mediation of expression, refuses the Cartesian tradition of self-knowledge.

Sartre has always rejected this knowledge of oneself in terms of the world as an alienation. In its place in his early work, Sartre adjusted for his purposes Husserl's phenomenological reduction. According to Sartre, to know oneself in terms of the world is bad faith, or seriousness, the materialist attitude. Only a purifyng reflection will allow consciousness to stand back and know itself as purified from contamination with its constituted products. In *Being and Nothingness* Sartre considered the natural attitude as something for which one is responsible, the natural attitude being a flight behavior, an attempt to hide what one knows to be true—that one is free. But it is precisely this clarity of the free consciousness to itself which is in question in making sense of alienation.

Sartre now proposes that it is a "necessity" for the agent to "initially" or "originally" discover itself in terms of its inscription in matter: "his objective perception of himself presents him as an inanimate object, the result of an operation" (*CDR* I, 227, n. 68). To make this possible there must be a diminution of self-consciousness: "Necessity, for man, is conceiving oneself originally as Other than one is and in the dimension of alterity. Certainly, *praxis* is self-explanatory [*se donne ses lumières*]; it is always conscious of itself. But non-thetic consciousness counts for nothing against the practical affirmation that *I* am what I have done" (*CDR* I, 227–28, n. 68). With Sartre's adoption of a *praxis* epistemology, he no longer speaks of a purifying reflection. His position is that an action comes to clarification in its performance: "the action, *in the course of its accomplishment*, provides its own clarification. . . . Then we will be able to account for the thought which is lost and alienated in the course of action so that it may be rediscovered by and in the action itself" (*SM*, 32–33). The agent's freedom would appear to the agent himself or herself in special circumstances of action. Sartre is not detailed on the nature of this self-discovery, but he manages to reverse the terms of his earlier thought. Whereas in his earlier, existentialist thought it was assumed that everybody "knew" about freedom, now, in order to account for alienation, it appears that everyone must "discover" freedom out of an initial alienation of knowledge. The issue is of the utmost consequence for a theory of responsibility, and it is distressing that Sartre does not linger on this change.

Thomas Flynn, in his *Sartre and Marxist Existentialism,* is one commentator who pays due attention to how the notions of self-awareness and comprehension play a pivotal role in Sartre's theory of responsibility. Flynn collapses the two notions: "comprehension is the self-awareness of praxis; there is no unconscious praxis,"[1] identifying the pre-reflective awareness of the early work with comprehension in the later work: "The epistemic primacy of praxis turns on Sartre's thesis that praxis is fully comprehensible to itself, a claim made on behalf of the pre-reflective *cogito* in his earlier work."[2] We have argued that, in fact, in the early work Sartre can be read as holding the view that no consciousness could avoid knowing that it was free.

Only this assumption could clarify why there were only two options presented in *Being and Nothingness,* bad faith (flight from freedom) and authenticity (acceptance of freedom). Because Flynn identifies the pre-reflective awareness of the early work with comprehension in the later, he argues that passive activity (alienation) is itself flight in the sense of bad faith. "In the language of existentialism, passive activity is basically flight from freedom-responsibility."3 The conclusion would logically follow, and Flynn draws it, that for Sartre in the end all people are equally responsible. Thus, little Genet would be in bad faith, as would the pariah, and the woman in the Dop shampoo factory. I have argued that Genet and the pariah are not classical cases of bad faith, but the appearance of a new species, as it were, and a challenge to the existentialism Sartre had built upon the *cogito.*

We have noticed that Sartre displaces self-awareness in order to account for alienation of knowledge when he writes that "non-thetic consciousness counts for nothing" against knowledge through externalization. If that is the case, how could one be guilty of fleeing freedom in the classic sense of bad faith? While it is true that Sartre calls comprehension the "transparency" of *praxis* to itself, does that mean that comprehension plays the same role in the later work as self-awareness in the earlier work? These questions will be addressed again when we take up the study of Flaubert, a work in which the problem of the alienation of knowledge is discussed in terms of a person's "pre-history." At this point, however, we can suggest that comprehension does not consistently play the role of the pre-reflective *cogito* in the early work. In the *Critique of Dialectical Reason* I, comprehension is tied to situation in a way that the Cartesian pre-reflective *cogito* was not. Flynn is aware of this and treats of it as "other-comprehension." He offers as an example: "Bourgeois humanism, for example, as a practico-inert idea, affects cognitive aspects of praxis."4 This appears to be an instance of Sartre's contention that class acts "as a limit of [one's] practical comprehension" (*CDR* I, 699), and is compatible with the assertion we observed him to make that comprehension is tied to "the position of the observer." Flynn is quick to recognize the difficulty this makes for Sartre's thought. If comprehension is limited to the grasp the bourgeois has of the bourgeois world and the silent understanding of bourgeois behavior across shared practices, values, etc., would the bourgeois comprehend that this bourgeois world is oppressive? Flynn argues that self-awareness must penetrate deeper than this social comprehension. "Yet even in the non-communication of other-comprehension there must remain the possibility of achieving more adequate awareness."5 His reason is that if there were not a "preideological . . . 'intimation of freedom' . . . presumably available to proletarian and bourgeois alike" it would not be possible for Sartre "to reserve a place for individual moral responsibility."6 These remarks are to the point in laying out a dilemma for Sartre's thought as it attempts to reconcile the power of consciousness and the force of circumstances. Flynn, however, concludes that comprehension must function as the pre-reflective *cogito* of the early work in order to fit in with his assumption that Sartre does, throughout his work, hold to the same views on freedom and responsibility. It is possible to agree with Flynn that "there must remain the possibility of achieving more adequate awareness" than other-comprehension. But this could be a painful learning process rather than an always available intuition, and if it is a learning process, responsibility would be proportionate to enlightenment.

<h3 style="text-align:center">SERIES/GROUP</h3>

Sartre begins his dialectical investigation, we have noted, with abstract individual *praxis:* "the individual is here only a methodological point of departure" (*CDR* I, 55). By tracing out individual *praxis* he will illuminate "through deeper and deeper conditioning, the totality of his bonds with others and, thereby, the structures of the various practical multitudes and, through their contradictions and struggles, 'the absolute concrete historical man'" (*CDR* I, 52). Concrete man, the singular universal, is thoroughly socialized, already dialectical, totalizing and totalized on multiple levels. Any analytic slice into a person's life will uncover a point of intersection between synchronic and diachronic factors of various ongoing totalizations. It is only in terms of concrete man or singular universal that it is possible to reconcile the Freudian and Marxist influences upon social conditioning and solidarity. After having failed to do this in *Saint Genet: Actor and Martyr,* Sartre will try again in *The Family Idiot.* From the perspective of concrete man, an individual is already socialized, from infancy: "For a man is never an individual; it would be more fitting to call him a *universal singular"* (*FI* I, ix). Thus in terms of dialectical intelligibility the individual is shot through with social and environmental relationships. Ontologically Sartre subscribes in *Critique of Dialectical Reason* I to "dialectical nominalism," holding that only individuals exist. We will reserve comment on this ontological individualism until our conclusion, in which we will take up Sartre's later use of the term "bifide."

The most prevalent social collection for Sartre is the series. The series is referred to as "massification," thus revealing its conceptual roots in the initial reflections on social phenomena in *The Communists and Peace.* By beginning his discussion of social phenomena with the series, Sartre tells us that he does not imply some actual historical developmental sequence: "it is no part of our project to determine whether series precede groups or vice versa" (*CDR* I, 65). His structural account will display the possibility for series to turn into groups and vice versa. While he admits the importance of the mode of production for understanding social structures such as series, "which express the fundamental social order (mode of production, relation of production, etc.)" (*CDR* I, 257), he once again turns from the usual Marxist methodology in favor of featuring the weight of mediating structures, as he had forecast in *Search for a Method.*

Serial relationships are atomistic, in the sense of being "a plurality of isolations," wherein individuals "exist side by side." These relationships, he tells us, lack "community." To display seriality, he employs the by now well-known example of people waiting for a bus. The unity of these individuals is exterior, their interest in the bus. Their relationship is passive since they submit to the etiquette of a people whose number may exceed available seating. Everyone is Other to each, since they are in competition for seats. "Their acts of waiting are not a communal fact, but are lived separately as identical instances of the same act" ((*CDR* I, 262).

Class being is seriality writ large. Individuals driven by need in a condition of scarcity employ means to survive which define their lives and relationships. Their very number puts them in competition for jobs and scarce commodities. The machines they work at, the division of labor, the working hours of the modern industrial workers, isolate them from one another. Thus isolation is social, not ontological: "their very isolation is a historical and social characteristic" (*CDR* I, 95). Their social relation *is* isolation and it is a product of the practico-inert. Finally, and this loomed as the most significant characteristic in our previous sketch of class, the relations are suffered passively. The activity of serial individuals is a transcendence-transcended, for within seriality individuals are destined to live in isolation, defined by the practico-inert, and suffer transcendence-transcended. The ray of hopefulness in *Critique of Dialectical Reason* I comes with the discussion of the possible passage from series to group. Again, this was presaged in *The Communists and Peace* when Sartre held out the possibility of enlarging freedom through group identification. In *Critique of Dialectical Reason* I Sartre explores in detail the condition of possibility for group action, and in doing this he tacitly reopens the question of social reality as it was presented in *Being and Nothingness*.

The persistent difficulty in Sartre's reflection on solidarity has been his phenomenological methodology, which dictates that relationships be found intelligible in terms of subject/object. Even as Sartre has turned to a dialectical method, this tendency to frame issues in terms of subject/object lingers. The totalizing/totalized relationship comes to be used synonymously with that of subject/object in discussing human relationships: "the free organization of the practical field presupposes a transcendence and it is impossible for the transcendence itself to feature in the field as transcended" (*CDR* I, 369); "a totalizing *praxis* cannot totalize itself as a totalized element" (*CDR* I, 373). No direct reciprocity is possible, and mediation is required. This of course is a position Sartre had taken in *Being and Nothingness*. The important difference from this previous position is that now Sartre uses for mediation a Third that is not other than the group. In fact each member of the group acts as a Third to the Others.

Every third party tends to become a mediation, as such, between the group and any other third party (or all of them). This is because I am not in fact alone in carrying out the totalizing operation, that is to say, in integrating the ensemble of individuals into the group and in revealing through my action the unity of a *praxis* which I produce and which produces itself. This operation is the individual and common *praxis* of *every third party* insofar as (failing to effect his real integration) he designates himself as free, common action becoming regulatory through him. From this point of view, I am, for every third party, a free human agent, but engaged (with other third parties and inside the group) in a constellation of mediated reciprocities. (*CDR* I, 579)

The new relationships established by these multiple mediations issue in "common freedom" and "common action." Sartre does not use the concept of "identification" in *Critique of Dialectical Reason* I that he had used in *The Communists and Peace,* preferring instead the term *same:* "Through the mediation of the group, he is neither the Other nor identical (identical with *me*): but he comes to the group as I do; he is the *same* as me" (*CDR* I, 377). The mediation is human and "interior" because it is *praxis.* Sartre thereby is consistent with his position in *The Communists and Peace* that community is not constituted only objectively: "Yet neither common need, nor common *praxis,* nor common objective can define a community unless it makes itself into a community by feeling individual need as common need, and by projecting itself, in the internal unification of a common integration, towards objectives which it produces as common" (*CDR* I, 550).

The transforming element, while interior, is not something reflectively decided. Conditions, Sartre indicates, must be ripe for a transfer from seriality to group. There must be a number of preceding mediations, as in his account of the forming of the group that stormed the Bastille. In Sartre's account, the motive for the group's formation was the perception, at an historical moment, "that the impossibility of change is an impossibility of life" (*CDR* I, 350). The major result of the overcoming of the passivity of serial existence is the "reorganization of human relations" and the "restoration of freedom."

The group-in-fusion appears on the scene as a temporary response to a fluid situation. To preserve the newly discovered human relations and freedom of the group, deliberate steps must be taken. Members of the group will consciously pledge themselves to the group, different roles will be created for the life the group, etc. As compared with Sartre's presentation of the group-in-fusion as pure *praxis,* the pledged group is an amalgam of activity and passivity, a passivity recognized and accepted. But once passivity enters the picture, it is possible that inertia will overtake the group, that it will become an institution and succumb to authoritarian unity.

The *Critique of Dialectical Reason* I is a valiant attempt to account for alienation and solidarity. Sartre, through his notion of practico-inert and counter-finality, gives a convincing account of how free actions are mediated by matter and affect agents. In terms of solidarity, *Critique of Dialectical Reason* I moves beyond *Being and Nothingness* by admitting the existence of a *We,* a common subjectivity: "Here there appears the first 'we' [*nous*], which is practical but not substantial, as the free ubiquity of the me as an inte-riorized multiplicity. It is not that I am myself in the Other: it is that in *praxis* there is no *Other,* there are only several *myselves*" (*CDR* I, 394–95). Sartre's account of community veers away from exploiting the social epistemology of the notion of comprehension which he introduced in *Search for a Method,* where comprehension implied a "lateral" awareness of being-with-Others in terms of shared practices. Instead, Sartre returns to his subject/object model. Nonetheless, his admission of the reality of community marks an important development in his thinking, one that became a preoccupation toward the end of his life, as we will see.

In other respects, *Critique of Dialectical Reason* I fails to follow up on the sensitivity toward mediation—the plurality of meanings, the focus upon the "between" instead of the terms of a relation—which were so evident in *Search for a Method.* Sartre's earlier dualistic tendencies resurface to contend with the newly emerging concern with mediations. Instead of maintaining the ambiguity of complexity, Sartre all too often in *Critique of Dialectical Reason* I is intent upon resolving complexity into types. The termminology of "pure *praxis*" and "pure exteriority" (*CDR* I, 247, 105), insinuates itself. His depiction of labor in terms of an organism externalizing itself in matter, becoming an inertia subject to the forces of worked-matter, smacks of the Manichean imagery of a Fall, and resuscitates the sharp boundaries of the early works between interiority and exteriority. While Sartre's phe-nomenology of the series has an undoubted ring of truth, it often comes across as an abstract type. The discussion of seriality seems oblivious to the various mediations Sartre condemned the Marxists for forgetting, media-tions that create different expressions of seriality, various expressions, for example, of acceptance, refusal, etc. Sartre seems to disdain the little refusals and rebellions that people create to "humanize" their situation. Their activity appears relegated to passive activity as opposed to pure *praxis,* which is exclusive of passivity: "In fact the free development of a *praxis* can only be total or as totally alienated" (*CDR* I, 395). This echoes his early, existentialist position that a human being is either totally free or a thing. For the most part Sartre appears uneasy with passivity, unable to accommodate it to *praxis.* The obvious exception is in the discussion of groups. The passivity of the group-in-fusion, in the form of objectification and totaliza-tion, is integrated into reciprocity, even in the means whereby that occurs through the Third: "the Other, by totalizing the practical community through his regulatory action, *effects for me* the integration which I myself should have realized, but was unable to" (*CDR* I, 379). In the pledged group one willingly assumes being a means, by virtue of admitting differen-tiation of functions and ideas, to keep the group in existence. These moments stand out from the general thrust of *Critique of Dialectical Reason* I, which holds that passivity and structures are alienating. The tension be-tween activity and passivity, and in general between the categories formerly built around the power of consciousness and those built around the force of circumstances, becomes even more heightened in the study of Flaubert which introduces the unsurpassable passivity of infancy.

THE FAMILY IDIOT

Sartre's massive (over 3,000 pages), and unfinished, study of Flaubert was to be a synthesis of existentialism, psychoanalysis, and Marxism, enabling him to express what can be known of a man at this point in history. From the perspective of our interest in social conditioning it is a pivotal text. Sartre resumes the attention to child development he began in the study of Genet, this time probing into the infancy period. With his claim that this period is decisive for later behavior, he reopens in another manner the question of the relationship of existentialism and Marxism to a psycho-analysis that seems to have assumed a priority over them.[7]

"We have our origins," Sartre proclaims, "in our prehistory" (*FI* I, 38). It is in Gustave Glaubert's prehistory, in this case his infancy, that Sartre discovers the appearance of the fundamental characteristic that threads its way throughout the spirals of his future development—*passivity*. It is the "essential element of his character" (*FI* I, 17). Sartre clearly blames Gustave's mother, Caroline, for his passive constitution: "It is certain . . . that his passivity comes from his mother and is the first internalization of the external world" (*FI* I, 375). By taking the position that fundamental character traits are established in infancy, Sartre moves beyond his previous positions on social alienation. In *Critique of Dialectical Reason* I Sartre put forth, very briefly and sketchily, a theory of the alienation of knowledge. We noted it as a displacement of self-consciousness in the development of a person's sense of self, for Sartre claimed that our original grasp of our-selves is mediated by externality. In fulfilling need, the agent impresses itself upon matter, transforming matter into a cultural product charac-terized by inertia, "so that his first knowledge of himself is knowledge of himself as inertia" (*CDR* I, 227). Sartre claims this initial mediation is "necessary" and the self-consciousness of *praxis* "counts for nothing" against it. In *Critique of Dialectical Reason* I he identifies "the foundation of necessity as practice" (*CDR* I, 227). This puts initial alienation in the result of labor— "the practical affirmation that *I* am what I have done" (*CDR* I, 229). Now in *The Family Idiot*, Sartre is moving the moment of alienation of knowledge of self from the practico-inert into the mother's behavior toward her infant. The initial alienation of knowledge is a social issue.

In the case of the particular relation between mother Caroline and infant Gustave, Sartre reconstructs what he is fairly sure happened. He offers a likely story. Caroline had badly wanted a daughter. She had one son, Achille, whose birth was subsequently followed by the birth and death of two more sons. Then came Gustave. Not only did she want a daughter,

Sartre surmises, but she expected Gustave to die. She did not abuse or despise Gustave, she "did what was necessary" (*FI* I, 127). She was "a mother out of duty" (*FI* I, 129). Gustave's every need was anticipated and met, but he was not loved. Two deadly and interconnected consequences ensued: his passivity and lack of self-esteem. They constituted Flaubert before he had a chance to defend himself.

> When a mother nurses or cleans an infant, she expresses, like everyone, her integrity of *self*, which naturally sums up her entire life from birth; at the same time she achieves a relationship that is variable according to circumstances and individuals—of which she is the *subject* and which can be called maternal love. I say that it is a relationship and not a feeling: indeed affection, properly speaking, translates itself into actions and is measured by them. But at the same time, by this love and through it, through the very person of the mother— skillful or clumsy, brutal or tender, such as her history has made her—*the child is made manifest to himself.* He learns his flesh through the pressures, the foreign contacts, the gropings, the bruisings that jostle him, or through a skillful gentleness. He will know his bodily parts, violent, gentle, beaten, constrained, or free through the violence or gentleness of the hands that awake him. . . . He internalizes the material rhythms and labors as qualities lived with his own body. (*FI* I, 47).

Gustave, in his infancy, "has been *made passive* by maternal attention" (*FI* I, 144). This occurs, of course, prior to any choice that Gustave might make about his life. This initial constitution leaves an indelible mark that will be taken up in various forms of totalization during Flaubert's life, but it will always be conserved and color the spirals of his life: "Preserved, surpassed, scored with new and complex meanings, this original sense cannot help being modified. But its modification *must be inclusive,* indeed it involves reproducing a new whole out of the internal contradictions of a previous totality and the project that was born of them" (*FI* I, 44).

Sartre claims that Gustave could have received countervailing responses from his father, Achille-Cléophas Flaubert, which could have conditioned oppositions within his character. Gustave's relations with his father, however, reinforced his passivity: "onto this internalized inertia an alien will is grafted" (*FI* I, 395). Achille-Cléophas Flaubert was of peasant origins, but through his medical skills he had been able to enter the bourgeois class. He conserved his peasant orientation toward family life, being strongly patriarchal. Gustave's older brother Achille was designated to become a surgeon, Gustave a lawyer. Achille was bright and eager to succeed. Gustave sensed the comparison made between him and his other brother. Would Gustave do as well? It became apparent that something was amiss when Gustave did not begin to read at the normal time. His father, whose expectations were being dashed, rejected Gustave, calling him "the family idiot." His judgment reinforced Gustave's passivity. Caroline had constituted her son a passive infant; Achille-Cléophas constituted his son a passive child. Gustave had no means, Sartre tells the reader, by which he could oppose his father's judgment, for he had internalized his passivity to the extent that he was incapable of the *praxis* of rebellion: "the passive child cannot even conceive the project of appropriating for himself the act of others by reaffirming the affirmation or denying it" (*FI* I, 156). Gustave sensed that his life was destined and that he had no power to do anything about it. He imagined himself already old, already dead.

Sartre's analysis of Flaubert's reading "problem" affords the opportunity to explore the nature of his passivity in more depth. Rejecting any suggestion of a physical impairment such as dyslexia, he proposes that the difficulty with reading was directly related to Gustave's passive constitution. Linguistic activity, in general, Sartre argues, is an activity which involves *praxis*, since the speaker, or reader, assumes the role of signifier. Gustave's passivity moved him to consider language something entirely other. Words were external things which named him. He spoke words but did not produce them. He could not internalize language to make it serve his purposes: "From the moment he must learn to read, language transforms itself before his eyes—he has to decompose, recompose according to the rules, affirm, deny, communicate; what he must be taught is not only the alphabet but *praxis* for which *nothing* has prepared him. The pathic child approaches *practice* and discovers he is not suited for it" (*FI* I, 39). The difficulties Gustave had with language stem from the fact that he "had a poor initial relation with the Other" (*FI* I, 14). This way of tying together language and social existence shows Sartre to be in substantial agreement with Ver Eecke and Aboulafia, who, as we have seen, emphasize the role of language and relationship with others in the child's development. In particular, they view the internalization of the negative as a crucial moment in the development of the child as an independent, active, self. In *The Family Idiot*, Sartre's thought comes to meet their objections. Indeed, Sartre tells us, speaking of Gustave: "this passive agent would not know how to achieve . . . negation through an act—such as radical refusal or revolt" (*FI* I, 226). Flaubert's sense of self has been shaped in such a way that he cannot assume the role of agent: "the passivity the child has internalized does not give him the tools that allow him to *recognize* this praxis" (*FI* I, 350). He "is estranged by the false consciousness of self imposed on him" (*FI* I, 496). Once again, we see the transparency of self-consciousness dimmed and displaced in order to allow for alienation. "Even on the level of non-thetic consciousness," Sartre claims, "intuition is conditioned by individual history" (*FI* I, 141). The study of Flaubert brings the probing of alienation to a new depth.

In their study of *Saint Genet: Actor and Martyr*, Laing and Cooper point out that Sartre fails to relate the phenomena of Genet's later life to his "early infantile life." Specifically they have in mind the issue of unconscious phantasy.

The material presented by Sartre falls readily into place in a psycho-analytic conceptual framework within which mechanisms such as introjective and projective identification, idealization of the object, denial and splitting operate. These mechanisms function in that realm of experience known as unconscious phantasy, and have their origin in early infantile life, to which, in the case of Genet, Sartre too often accords only an implicit and unsystematic recognition.[8]

Laing and Cooper suggest that early phantasies may be regarded as part of one's facticity, but in that case, "To what extent is one free to choose oneself, in the face of phantasies which seem to determine one's perception of oneself and of others, and which originate in a phase that is ontogenetically prior to responsibility in the ordinary sense of the term?"[9] By incorporating "prehistory" into his study of Flaubert, Sartre does thereby grant an integral part of the intelligibility of the force of circumstances to this ontogenetically prior phase, giving an urgency to the question posed by Laing and Cooper. Can Sartre claim now, as he had in *Critique of Dialectical Reason* I, that "existential principles remain unaffected?"

It is clear that the discourse of *The Family Idiot* is a mixed one. Sartre speaks of the making of Flaubert, as we have been observing; on the other hand he insists that Flaubert is not determined. And in order to make his point, Sartre employs the discourse of activity. Gustave exhibits passive activity.

> Passivity is his lot, but he is a child of man, not an idiot, not even a wild child; like all men, he is a surpassing, a project; he *can* act. (*FI* I, 39)

> In fact, Gustave *will not choose* passive action among other equally possible modes of praxis; rather the praxis itself is produced as the internal work of inertia when it is impossible for it not to exist. . . . Praxis becomes the *efficacy of the passive* because the child's conditioning strips him of any means of affirming himself, even the positive act of negativity. (*FI* I, 139)

Passivity, if it is to exist, must be made to be ("passivity *does not simply exist;* it must continually create itself, (*FI* I, 42). The crucial event at *Pont-L'Évêques* offers an opportunity to watch Sartre use this discourse of passive activity. On a January evening in 1844 Gustave and Achille were riding in a carriage. Gustave was driving.

> Suddenly, in the vicinity of Pont-L'Évêques, a wagon passed to the right of the carriage; Gustave dropped the reins and fell thunderstruck at his brother's feet. Seeing his corpselike immobility, Achille believed him to be dead or dying. In the distance the lights of a house were seen. The elder son carried the younger there and urgently took care of him. Gustave remained for a few minutes in this cataleptic state; he did, however, retain his full consciousness. When he opened his eyes, did he have convulsions or not? It is difficult to know. In any case his brother took him to Rouen the same night. (*IF* 2, 721)[10]

At this point in his life Gustave felt trapped in a dead end. He wanted to be an artist, not a lawyer, and his father was fiercely opposed. He had failed his law examination and was soon to retake it. He did not want to fail and disgrace the family and he could not, because of his passive constitution, disobey his father. As in the case with the reading problem, Sartre refuses to consider the episode as a neurophysiological illness. It was an "appropriate" illness, for as a result of it, Gustave was not able to continue with his legal studies and, being considered now an invalid, had the leisure to write. In broad outlines, Sartre's depiction of the "spell" is reminiscent of his earlier account of hysteria in *The Emotions: Outline of a Theory*.[11] But there are, I believe, crucial differences, owing to the displacement of the *cogito*. *The Family Idiot* carries on the displacement of the *cogito*, or more precisely, the non-thetic self-consciousness, and this must be taken into account here. His claim that "even on the level of non-thetic self-consciousness, intuition is conditioned by individual history" (*FI* I, 141) is a deeper probing of the admission in *Critique of Dialectical Reason* I of those alienating situations in which the non-thetic self-consciousness "counts for nothing." In bold contrast stands his earlier Cartesian view which so heavily weighted the non-thetic self-consciousness and led him so easily to accusations of bad faith. Recall his assertion of how readily the oppressed grasp their freedom: "they attain themselves immediately, by non-thetic self-consciousness, which envelops an ontological comprehension of existence as absolute subjectivity" (*C*, 488). According to Sartre's account of Gustave's conditioning, the latter interprets his conscious life in terms of the categories provided by his social environment. Concrete (as opposed to metaphysical) freedom depends on self-concept. Sartre characterizes Gustave's early stupors or ekstatic trances, as well as his inability to read, as "first unconscious ventures" (*FI* I, 15), "intentional" and "spontaneous" (*FI* I, 23), "neither conscious nor voluntary" (*FI* I, 23). The event on the bridge is "only their radicalization" (*FI* I, 349). The episode was intentional; that is, it made sense in terms of its context; but it was not a case of *praxis*, a result of choosing the most economical means from a field of possibilities, in order to realize an end. The essence of passive activity is disguise: "Passive activity attains its ends only so that this may be kept hidden from the agent; so as to have lived this obscurely as the internal structures of passivity" (*IF* 2, 1687–88). Again, "these intentions can modify the course of experience only on condition of not being recognized; that is, of disguising their reality and their significance" (*IF* 2, 1688). They are "necessarily hushed up" ("necessairement etouffé"; *IF* 2, 1141). Human behavior always means, signifies. The intentionality of passive action adjusts itself to a situation in seeking equilibrium. Gustave's childhood silences, his "stupors," are interpreted by Sartre as "precisely a refusal to grow up" (*FI* I, 343). The inability to read is "the refusal to become an adult" (*FI* I, 344), a "self-defense," a "strategem." By depicting passive activity as intentional, Sartre is consistent with his existentialist refusal to reduce human agency to mechanistic explanations. But is he consistent with the options offered by his existentialist ontology according to which human reality "is wholly and forever free or . . . is not free at all?" (BN, 441). He does insist that "the passive agent, though alienated, remains free" (IF 2, 1689). Does this imply that Gustave's strategies are chosen, and even forms of bad faith, conforming to his existentialist options in Being and Nothingness: one is either in bad faith or authentic? If the answer is affirmative, then Sartre would exemplify the intellectualist (rationalist) described by Merleau-Ponty:

> If consciousness is placed outside being, the latter cannot break it; the empirical variety of consciousnesses—morbid, primitive, childlike consciousness, the consciousness of Others—cannot be taken seriously, there is nothing to be known or understood, one thing alone makes sense: the pure essence of consciousness. None of these consciousnesses could fail to effect the Cogito. The lunatic behind his ravings, his obsession and lies, knows that he is raving, that he is allowing himself to be haunted by an obsession, that he is lying, in short he is not mad.[12]

My view is that, from the Genet study on, Sartre had indeed been taking seriously "the empirical variety of consciousnesses," the infant, the child, the pariah, the neurotic. His analysis of passive activity in terms of an intentionality below consciousness, or at least only obscurely felt, sounds very·much like Merleau-Ponty's prepersonal psychosomatic intentionality. In discussing the case of a young girl who lost her voice after being forbidden to see her lover, Merleau-Ponty writes:

> Of course we may go on to speak of hypocrisy or bad faith. But then it will be necessary to draw a distinction between psychological and metaphysical hypocrisy. The former deceives others by concealing from them thoughts expressly in the mind of the subject. It is fortuitous and easily avoided. The latter is self-deceiving through the medium of generality, thus leading finally to a state or a situation which is not an inevitability, but which is not posited or voluntary.[13]

Merleau-Ponty's reference to "the medium of generality" in this context is to the role played in intentional behavior by the body, as he non-dualistically conceives of it. There are indications throughout The Family Idiot, principally in his use of "somatization," that Sartre is adopting a similar position. From the extraordinary influence Sartre places upon the initial instances of an infant's being touched to the stress he puts on Gustave's headaches, fatigue, ennui, he shows an increasing appreciation for the psychosomatic integrity of human reality. Unfortunately, he never pauses to elaborate clearly any of these conceptual tools, nor to compare them with his existentialist ontology, which is apparently still operative for him.

In several interviews subsequent to the publication of *The Family Idiot,* Sartre commented upon the conceptual difference between *The Family Idiot* and his previous works. He recognizes now what he calls "those processes which are 'below' consciousness" (*BEMIT,* 41), also claiming that in *The Family Idiot* the very notion of "experience" has changed in order to incorporate this recognition: "What I call *le vécu*—lived experience—is precisely the ensemble of the dialectical process of psychic life, insofar as this process is obscure to itself because it is a constant totalization, thus necessarily a totalization which cannot be conscious of itself: (*BEMIT,* 41). Lived experience is "the equivalent of conscious-unconscious. I want to give the idea of a whole whose surface is completely conscious, while the rest is opaque to this consciousness and, without being part of the consciousness, is hidden from view" (*IF-L/S,* 127). Sartre refuses to separate the unconsious from consciousness and to propose a system of external "mechanical" relationship between them. He incorporates the "unconscious" into consciousness as an "opaque" and "hidden from view" dimension of consciousness. He insists that consciousness is still self-consciousness (" 'lived experience' represents an effort to preserve that presence to itself which seems to me indispensible for the existence of any psychic fact"), but, in deference to the displacement of self-consciousness that is necessary to account for social alienation, he limits the extent of self-consciousness, "while at the same time this presence is so opaque and blind before itself that it is also an absence from itself. Lived experience is always simultaneously present to itself and absent from itself" (*BEMIT,* 42). This concept is pivotal to the integrity of Sartre's thought, for it marks an attempt to reconcile the two different discourses— the power of consciousness and the force of circumstances—that characterize the body of Sartre's work. He employs the term "preserve" when referring to "presence to self," indicating his awareness of conserving an element of his previous thought, while now introducing the new element of "absence," claiming to hold them "simultaneously" in a new synthesis and totalization of thought. Unfortunately, he does no more than introduce the concept, and, crucial as it is to the integrity of his thought, does not explicate it. In 1971 he admitted: "The notion of experience is a tool I use, but one I have not theorized" (*IF-L/S,* 128). I know of no place after that where he added more to what had been said by then.

In one of the relevant interviews, he links the notion of lived experience to that of intentionality in a way that bears on *The Family Idiot.*

Every psychic fact involves an intentionality which aims at something, while among them a certain number can only exist if they are comprehended, but neither named nor known. The latter includes what I call the "stress" of a neurosis. A neurosis is in the first instance a specific wound, a defective structure which is a certain way of living a childhood. But this is only the initial wound: it is then patched up and bandaged by a system which covers and soothes the wound, and which then, like antibodies in certain cases, suddenly does something abominable to the organism. The unity of this system is the neurosis. The work of its "stress" is intentional, but it cannot be seized without disappearing. It is precisely for this reason that if it is transferred into the domain of knowledge, by analytic treatment, it can no longer be reproduced in the same manner. (*BEMIT,* 42)

There is a "wound," a passivity, which is then "patched up and bandaged" by activity. The "stress" would be the attempt to help the system to effect equilibrium. But the "stress" cannot be "seized," i.e., it keeps itself hidden. This is an apt depiction of the "intentionality," which is neither conscious nor elective, used in *The Family Idiot* to explicate Flaubert's seizure at Pont-L'Évêques, his stupor, his failure to read. Commenting on the above passage, Hazel Barnes in her book *Sartre* (1973) writes: "we have here still the bad faith which Sartre spoke of so many years before, the lie to oneself."[14] She appears to agree with Flynn's contention that passive activity, as defined in the later work, is synonymous with the analysis of flight behavior outlined in *Being and Nothingness*. In her book *Sartre and Flaubert* (1981), she offers a more nuanced interpretation of the described behavior. She allows that the original "will to fail" might be a form of bad faith, but the "hiding" of the original "decision" as depicted in *The Family Idiot* is something new. It is the "subsequent nonconscious development of a repressed decision which is quite different from anything found in *Being and Nothingness*."[15] It is true that the discourse on neurosis (patching, soothing, hiding), while it is a discourse of activity, would have to be identified conceptually with the lucidity of self-consciousness of the early works in order to equate the linkage to the bad faith of *Being and Nothingness*. Her position implies something that is not clearly stated in the text, however; namely, that there are two distinct moments in the neurosis: an original lucid decision, followed by a non-conscious cover-up. In Flaubert's case, it is unclear how he is able to repress a decision (lucid enough for bad faith) which, according to Sartre's account of his passivity, he has no means to recognize, since he thinks that events happen to him. In *Being and Nothingness* Sartre insisted that one can only hide in bad faith what one already knows. In *Being and Nothingness*, there was no developmental theory of the sense of self, its assumption being that everyone really knows he or she is free and that what follows is either a cover-up or an acceptance. But if one form of alienation is an "alienation of knowledge," then it must be admitted that not all people have the free and active sense of self that is required for bad faith. In *Adieux*, Sartre tells Simone de Beauvoir that he always "feels free" but he recognizes the role of his upbringing in that feeling, and he realizes that others do not have the same feeling, thereby admitting *degrees of awareness of freedom:* "And I think that all other men are like me, but that the degree of awareness and the clarity with which this freedom appears to them varies according to the circumstances, according to their origins, their development, and their knowledge" (*A,* 361). He refers to "that confused state of mind that men have with regard to their freedom" (*A, 36o*), and a "muddling" of minds through which "freedom of thought and action is confused . . . and hidden by collective images, by repetitive actions performed every day under constraint by conceptions that have been learned, not thought out by themselves, and by a lack of knowledge" (*A, 36o*). If the sense of self as free agent is indeed mediated, it explains why there can be "lost" people, *victims of alienation in different degrees:* "it is obvious . . . that there is an enormous variation between different kinds of alienation: take, for example, autistic children or Wolf children" (*IF-L/S,* 116), or the pariah Genet, or Gustave Flaubert, etc. While Sartre continues to hold that ontologically all human beings are free, he does not continue to hold that all human beings inescapably realize that they are free. Bad faith in its classic sense remains a valid analysis of the human being with a developed sense of self as active and free, who then tries to flee freedom. But victims of alienation, according to Sartre, do not initially have this sense of self. It is true that in the interviews after the publication of *The Family Idiot,* Sartre allows that there is a comprehension of the "unconsious." He alters his previous definition of comprehension, however, as he proceeds to elaborate his meaning. In *Search for a Method* and *Critique of Dialectical Reason* I Sartre had defined comprehension as the transparency of *praxis;* specifically, he identified it as the recognition of intentionality as its *savoir.* He reserved the term "intellection" for those cases of action without an agent, the unintended consequence of action. But in the interviews touching on lived experience, he states: "I distinguish here between comprehension and intellection: there can be intellection of a practical conduct, but only comprehension of a passion" (*BEMIT,* 41), distinguishing comprehension from any form of cognition by relating it to affection. "A totalization which also totalizes consciousness" is *suffered* obscurely. While it is a "total absence of knowlege," comprehension can express itself, can forge its own language. Dreams are an example of such a language: "The highest form of comprehension of lived experience can forge its own language—which will always be inadequate, and yet which will often have the metaphysical structure of the dream itself. Comprehension of a dream occurs when a man can express it in a language which is itself dreamt" (*BEMIT,* 41). Comprehension, in this sense, could only be incorporated into the sense of self required for bad faith if it could reach a level of reflectivity such that it could be reacted to by the self in terms of producing a new totalization. If the self suffers a past experience which expresses itself in phantasies, it is only through understanding the phantasies and their function that the self could come to any degree of responsibility toward these expressions or their underlying motivation. Sartre's brief remarks on lived experience and comprehension are the latest in a line of evolving discourses on self-consciousness. In the early, existentialist period, non-positional self-consciousness, a Cartesian legacy, poisoned the intentional thrust toward identity with objects, throwing consciousness back upon itself and, in effect, creating a self/other dualism. Thus the self, or subject, was aware of its differentiation from objects and this served as the apparent reason for the self's sense of indetermination. Later, non-positional self-consciousness was displaced ("counts for nothing") in order to account for the "alienation of knowledge" needed to explain the "Genet" phenomenon and class consciousness. "Comprehension" appeared in tandem with *praxis* as the practical grasp of the self and Others in terms of, and across, the concrete situation. Now lived experience enters as a further displacement of the *cogito,* allowing for an "absence" and "obscurity" in self-apprehension. Comprehension of lived experience, in turn, is indirect, through expression and signs. Sartre never pauses to thematize these changes, however; they come and go without much comment, emerging as he needs them under the pressure of rendering intelligible the conditioned consciousness.

The possibility that objectification, passivity, and structures could be salvific arises in *The Family Idiot.* In turning from the *cogito* toward mediation in accounting for the self's sense of freedom and *praxis,* Sartre can be seen to grant an enabling role to externalization or objectification: "the love of the Other is the foundation and guarantee of the objectivity of the individual's value and his mission; this mission becomes a sovereign choice, permitted and evoked in the subjective person by the presence of self-worth" (*FI* I, 135). The infant needs to be *valorized,* to internalize a sense of being worthwhile, and encouraged to act. This result is a sense of mission through which the individual receives a sense of self and of self's actions as of consequence: "Without a particular mission he is deprived, *from the start,* of the cardinal categories of praxis. . . . To love life, to wait each minute for the next with confidence, with hope, one has to have been able to internalize the Other's love as a fundamental affirmation of the self" (*FI* I, 136, 392). The grasp of oneself in terms of externalization or objectification in writings previous to *The Family Idiot* was referred to as an alienation of knowledge. While he has never identified objectification and externalization as inherently alienating, Sartre has not developed a positive theory of either concept. In *Critique of Dialectical Reason* I, we saw one instance—the groups in which, through being totalized by the Third, one's freedom of action is enhanced. However, the main thrust of *Critique of Dialectical Reason* I was that externalization looms as a threat. Structures, the instituted or sedimented in general, were traps for *praxis.* In discussing the mother/infant relationship, Sartre has shown how the result was alienating in Gustave's case, but in doing this he tacitly pointed out the benefit of positive objectifying relations. The infant *needs* love, an objectification that would enable it to develop a sense of self as free *praxis.* Innocuous as it may appear, this admission by Sartre is significant for his project of understanding the conditioned consciousness and subjectivity itself. First, as a continuation of the exploration of childhood and development of self begun in the Genet book, it reveals a deeper understanding of facticity. By thematizing the "pre-conscious" original stage of development, Sartre is offering a sketch of the emergence of subjectivity in terms of a concrete sense of self upon which actions and attitudes depend. Second, Sartre is acknowledging not simply the inevitable stage of infancy and its permanent effects in the spiral of a life but the positive role of objectification in the loving handling of the infant by the mother. The infant requires love, valorization, to develop into a subject capable of *praxis*. There is here no longer the Cartesion foundationalism of self-production through doubt and *cogito,* no Husserlian reduction of meaning and value to oneself. Engagement in *praxis* itself depends to a great extent upon early life events beyond one's control.

Thus, in his pursuit of an account of the socially alienated consciousness, Sartre comes to the realization that all consciousness is inevitably conditioned, that the emergence of the subject is not guaranteed by the *cogito,* that the exercise of a free and critical attitude (embodied in his ontological notion of being-for-itself) must *emerge* through a certain "fitting" development. Thus alterity, in our earliest relations with the Other, is formative of the self, for good or ill. There is an implied ethic in Sartre's discussion of the infant's relations with Others, which surfaces now and again, but is not thematic: "Indeed, the Other is there, diffused, from the first day in the discovery I made of myself through my passive experience of otherness" (*FI* I, 129). After this acknowledgment of the inevitable presence of the Other in mediating self-apprehension, Sartre warns that on this basic level "love is required" and then asserts: "It is fitting in these moments that the child, discovering himself by and for this diffuse otherness, should apprehend himself in an external and internal ambiance of kindness" (*FI* I, 129). Nonetheless, one way or the other, infancy will be conserved into the future, as a passivity suffered and as an "inertia" conserved: "Emotional inertia" is a "being there . . . pure receptivity," which is "absorbed" in being taken up in passive action, and serves as a *means,* albeit limiting means, in any totalizing project. "Preserved, surpassed, scored with new and complex meanings, this original sense cannot help being modified. But its modification *must be inclusive,* indeed it involves reproducing a new whole out of the internal contradictions of a previous totality and the project that was born of them" (*FI* I, 43–44). This text expresses and develops admirably the sense of mediation, internal coloration, and negation-as-conserving that was recognized in *Search for a Method* and apparently forgotten in *Critique of Dialectical Reason* I. The language of "integration," "evolves," "transformed," "recomposed," "preserves," "scored," "modified," replaces the discourse of "contradiction," "instant," "fissure," "rupture," "creation" which dominates the early work. The language forms around the notion of totalization and signals a shift in underlying paradigm. This shift will constitute the focus of our next chapter.

The thrust of *Search for a Method, Critique of Dialectical Reason* I, and *The Family Idiot* in their creation of concepts to account for social alienation and solidarity has been to move Sartre's thought from dichotomous terms to mediation, the between, and relationships. The fruition of these works is the acceptance of the *We* and the model for thinking of a life as totalization. This has not taken place without tension, for, as we have seen, Sartre's dualistic tendencies were quite noticeable in *Critique of Dialectical Reason* I and traces are also apparent in *The Family Idiot*. Sartre often presents Gustave as utterly incapable of *praxis:* "Read the *Correspondence* from start to finish, never will you catch Flaubert judging, reasoning, making a critical examination; never will you find the birth of an idea, a new perception, an original point of view. In Flaubert, thought is never an *act;* it invents nothing" (*FI* I, 625). Thus Flaubert becomes a type. While Flaubert might never engage in *praxis* as an activity that would aim at changing his situation, he does engage in various recognizable forms of *praxis* in its usual sense, such as writing books, conversing, studying law, etc. When he excludes Gustave from *praxis,* the Cartesian notion of a "pure praxis" looms as a possibility. Yet, slowly, almost painstakingly, the recognition of alterity, objectification, and passivity as inevitable dimensions of the human self, and enabling and positive dimensions in many instances, has been growing in Sartre's texts. In *Critique of Dialectical Reason* I individual consciousnesses needed one another in their integration into the group. Also, the pledged group arose by virtue of a decision to use one's objectification for the group's purposes. Then, in *The Family Idiot,* there is infancy and childhood. The very ideas of infancy and childhood in the context of totalization mean that to be human is to have passivities, inertias. At times Sartre speaks of this as a gloomy truth. In an interview on *The Family Idiot,* he declared that "we are all lost during childhood. Methods of education, the parent-child relationship, and so on, are what create the self, but it's a lost self" (*IF-L/S,* 116), apparently forgetting his claim that only a loving valorization of an infant could enable it to assume *praxis.* That is clearly not a loss but a gain. It is true, of course, that human relationships (such as mother/infant) are being continually totalized by the various practico-inert structures of society. These structures are "mediating" rather than determining, for after all mothers from any class can give their children the initial love Sartre finds "fitting." Educational as well as other institutions can be stifling, as we know well from *Critique of Dialectical Reason* I. By embracing the developmental model of the self in *The Family Idiot,* however, Sartre clearly accepts also that the self is intrinsically social, for self-concept (and we have seen how crucial this is) is formed through relationships. For the developmental social self, Others and social arrangements in general are not inherently alienating. It is a question of hitting upon and sustaining those relationships that are "fitting." While Sartre originally accounted for alienation by introducing passivity or inertia into the self, it turns out that everyone's life is an admixture of activity and passivity. The seemingly pessimistic conclusion of this discovery is offset by the growing awareness that passivity and inertia can be enabling as well as alienating.

FIVE

Transformation

André Gorz, commenting on the relationship between *Being and Nothingness* and *Critique of Dialectical Reason* I, writes: "After having accounted for the *formal possibility* of alienation, it is a question of accounting for its *real existence*."[1] Gorz sees a continuous line of development between the two works in terms of an abstract set of conditions of possibility and the concrete, historical instantiation of that set. The difficulty with this view is that it does not sufficiently allow for the change in the concept of alienation from the earlier to the later work. In *Being and Nothingness,* bad faith was presented as flight, a sort of self-alienation, through which a person tried to hide his or her freedom, a freedom inescapably known. *Critique of Dialectical Reason* I, as a result of the expanding awareness on Sartre's part of social alienation, which we have traced out beginning with the inaugural editorial in *Les Temp Modernes,* offers two forms of social alienation. In one form, a free action, due to the mediation of the practical field, comes to take on unintended, even adverse consequences. In the other form, there is an alienation of knowledge, whereby an agent comes to interpret itself in terms of its inertia and objectification. As expanded in *The Family Idiot,* this type of alienation appears first in infancy and is seen to contain ineradicable consequences for one's life, as exemplified by Gustave's passive constitution. Each type of alienation belongs to a cluster of concepts of which it forms an intelligible part. For bad faith, it is a question of individuality, unconditioned freedom, lucidity, exclusory bifurcations of spontaneity/ inertia, internal/external, subject/object, activity/passivity, self/Others, pure/impure reflection. For the forms of social alienation it is dialectic, internalization and externalization, totalization, mediation, coloration, ambiguity, *praxis.* We frequently noted discrepancies between the latter and former sets of categories. One indication of a significant shift from early to late work involves Sartre's methodology, which begins with a static phenomenology and ends with a deep commitment to an historical and developmental perspective. The aim of Sartre's phenomenology was to discover, through description, invariant modes of being and conditions of possibility. In the later work phenomenology is situated as a moment between regressive and progressive analyses which contextualize eidetic intuition. We have observed Sartre to say that "*L'Être et Le Néant* traced an interior experience, without any coordination with the exterior experience of a petty-bourgeois intellectual." The linkage, the "coordination," between the interior and the exterior, is the focus of Sartre's dialectic, culminating in the notion of totalization employed in *The Family Idiot.*

While Sartre employs totalization as a working model for understanding a human life throughout *The Family Idiot,* he pauses only briefly to consider it explicitly in a few pages at the beginning of the section on "Personalization," which is his final statement on self-production. His remarks, particularly his language, are a significant point of comparison for later and earlier categories. He retains the early and pivotal concept of intentionality, conceiving it as a totalizing process, instead of a "rupture," "contradiction," or "break in being." "Perpetual totalization," he writes, is "an intentional and directed enterprise of unification" (*FI* II, 3). A psychosomatic organism tends toward a level of integrity or equilibrium in terms of satisfying physical needs and in terms of maintaining a level of unified experience. The concept of equilibrium has its roots in the introduction of the *needs* of concrete human reality in *Search for a Method* and *Critique of Dialectical Reason* I and it takes on an ever greater weight in his later thought. His most thoughtful and extensive treatment of equilibrium appears in *Critique de la raison dialectique* II, when he returns to probe the materiality of human reality, which is treated in the context of organic materiality as such. He refers to the "irreducible materiality which characterizes the agent" (*CDR* II, 317). This materiality is now called the "being-in-itself" of *praxis;* "the being-in-itself of praxis-process is what one could call its unassimilable and non-recuperable reality," constituting its "exterior limit" (*CDR* II, 319). The human organism itself is a "system," "a unity which produces itself" (*CDR* II, 314). Organic unity synthesizes physical and chemical elements, which form the necessary conditions of the system and which mark its fragility and mortality—its "exterior limit." The living system's unity is neither an established substantial unity nor a unity as an ideal to be realized. It is a unity "en cours," continually established and continually threatened: "In organic unity, in effect, what is found is neither a Unity-as-being nor a Unity-as-future-object-of-an-act, but rather an identity of Unity as ontological state and of Unity as perpetual reparation of damages" (*CDR* II, 355). The organism, impelled outside by its needs, tends toward preserving its unity by meeting its needs. Through a cycle of need and action on the environment to fulfill its needs, the organism aims at an equilibrium, a "provisional stability" (*CDR* II, 351), an "organic integrity" (*CDR* II, 381). The human organism invents tools and more sophisticated technology to adapt the environment to itself, and vice versa, in meeting needs. These fabrications are continually invented, bettered, discarded, etc., under the pressure of the changing environment. The materiality of the organism, its susceptibility to manipulation as well as the material variability of the environment, become the *means* of meeting needs: "*through* its inert being by inertia it works" (*CDR* II, 390). What is new is the emphasis upon success or partial success in maintaining a state of unity which is neither pure spontaneity nor pure inertia. Needs *can be* satisfied, syntheses can be successful; otherwise organic life would be impossible. The universe, Sartre admits, "tolerates" us. As Ronald Aronson notes,[2] materiality in the form of body, tools, language, the practico-inert in general, is not looked upon simply in the Manichean tone of *Critique of Dialectical Reason* I. Rather, the practico-inert is seen as enabling means to achieve the satisfaction of needs.

The view that an organism is an intentionality toward integrity or equilibrium, so prominently introduced in *Critique de la raison dialectique* II, is taken up on the psychosomatic level in *The Family Idiot*. The totalizing and retotalizing processes involve the familiar internalizing and externalizing of the dialectic, and surpassing as conservation. What is new is the notion of totalization as a level of psychic unity or equilibrium on the analogy of organic unity. There exists "an organic and always threatened unity that experience attains and maintains as it rolls along, like a snowball constantly increasing in size" (*FI* II, 4). A totalizing experience is constantly put into question by new life experience, or as Sartre in his inimitable way puts it, by "cosmic aggression" (*FI* II, 4). A totalization, under the impact of new experience, can produce a new synthesis, a retotalization, which would produce a unity capable of incorporating without contradiction the new experiences.

A totalization of experience must encounter and interpret any new experiences ("introduction of a foreign element," *FI* II, 4) in terms of the familiar, for "a synthetic activity . . . can comprehend and resolve problems only insofar as it is directed and limited by the concrete totality of the determinations it preserves within it" (*FI* II, 4). Again, "the danger is interpreted on the basis of affective and conjectural presuppositions that the individual has collected along the way and the options that have surpassed and maintained them" (*FI* II, 4). The tendency of the psychic organism is to maintain its integrity or present level of unity and "to prevent the new (the foreign) from jeopardizing that unity" (*FI* II, 3, 4). Sartre singles out three types of solution to the struggle to maintain equilibrium.

In one case the new experience, unassimilable in terms of present presuppositions and categories, can evoke a "transformation, . . . an effort to reduce the contradictions by acting on the whole so that to some degree it might integrate the new element as one of its parts" (*FI* II, 4). Second, one can "integrate" the new element into one's present totalization only on the basis of "belief," so that the contradictions really remain. Third, one can "subordinate" the unassimilable element by "an imaginary forgetting" (*FI* II, 5), which could take the form of projection or of introjection. The project of maintaining present unity and "forgetting" the new is "stress."

"Stress is the name we shall give to this unity of the nonassimilable element and the global defense that the process develops against it" (*FI* II, 5).

These limited provocative remarks comprise a new discourse on freedom, for they outline possible paths of retotalization. In commenting upon them, Hazel Barnes reminds us of the earlier notion of "choice of being" and "bad faith."[3] But we must be careful. Certain similarities are indeed suggested between "transformation" and "choice of being" or original project, and between "bad faith" and "imaginative forgetting," but there is no identity. Sartre's own explication of totalization and retotalization is itself a retotalization of his own earlier existentialist totalization. His retotalization is hermeneutic rather than Cartesian. In terms of the discourse of freedom, "transformation" is the most helpful of the three responses, but any transformation is itself dependent upon the options present in the previous totalization: "according to the specific character of these options, the totalizing reaction can be affected by the transformation of the collectivity to be totalized" (*FI* II, 4). The developmental model substitutes language of "evolution" ("the movement of personalizing evolution," *FI* II, 7) for that of the "instant" and unconditioned project. "The idea of an instant and total liberation is a utopia" (*BEMIT*, 61). Personalization follows upon constitution and is defined as "nothing more than the surpassing and preservation (assumption and inner negation) at the core of a project to totalize what the world has made—and continues to make—of us" (*FI* II, 7). The three types of personalization involve the conservation of an "archaic sense" which reaches back into organic constitution and infancy, and marks all personalization, including any "transformation." "Finally, when the inertia is entirely absorbed by the resulting *praxis* and is recomposed as the union of endured feeling and passive action, it will still preserve its archaic sense, just as the spear preserves the substance of the pole it once was" (*FI* I, 44).

The discourse of totalization in *The Family Idiot* is humanistic in the sense that it continues the early works' refusal to reduce the human existent to a mechanism or thing, but it avoids embracing the only other alternative of the early work—radical, unconditioned freedom. The discourse of *The Family Idiot* is primarily one of an intentionality seeking equilibrium, defined not as a state of inertia but as a *"perpetuum mobile,"* a type of constancy-in-motion. The triumphal tone of freedom, muted gradually through the course of Sartre's writings, is scarcely heard in *The Family Idiot*. Publicly, after *The Family Idiot*, Sartre continued his commitment to freedom, but in language quite different from that of his former pronouncements. "This is the limit I would today accord to freedom: the small movement which makes of a totally conditioned being someone who does not render back completely what his conditioning has given him" (*BEMIT*, 35). In fact, this can be considered the bottom line view of freedom that emerged after Sartre's recognition and probing of the "force of circumstances." Sartre's position in *The Family Idiot* is that Flaubert did not have to become the author of *Madame Bovary* in any necessary sense. Yet, in creating the story of Gustave's life, he argued that Gustave was formed into a "passivity" that prevented him from transforming his life through *praxis*. Flaubert was stuck, as it were, with the project of maintaining an equilibrium by neurosis. For some people, victims of a certain kind of infancy, stress is the only possible solution. "Dangerous as such stress may be, however, it nonetheless offers a way of surpassing the disturbing element" (*FI* II, 6). But the "imaginative forgetting" implied in stress is not identical to the earlier notion of bad faith, since the latter requires a knowledge of what one is denying. "Forgetting" is intentional, but in what sense is it free? Once again, the question posed by Laing and Cooper regarding the relation between freedom and "mechanisms such as introjective and projective identification, idealization of the object, denial and splitting . . . mechanisms which function in that realm of experience known as unconscious phantasy, and have their origin in early infantile life,"[4] is relevant. Sartre touches on the issue, but does not linger and analyze: "The most frequent result, however, is that the mere presence of the nonassimilable element generates antagonistic real elements which pounce on the nonassimilable one, attacking it and attempting to reduce it to impotence" (*FI* II, 5). Within the context of the importance Sartre attaches to *equilibrium*, as well as his willingness to use this notion equally of organic behavior and of experience, it is possible to view the "mechanisms" referred to in psychoanalysis as products of the intentional tendency toward, and desire for, equilibrium in situations where it cannot be effectively realized. "Belief" and "stress" reflect what Merleau-Ponty labeled "substitute" behavior, such as is observable in the adaptive behavior of the injured organism. This behavior is meaningful, but, to repeat, any talk of it as "chosen" or "bad faith" is out of place where sufficient lucidity on the agent's part is lacking. Sartre is driven in his pursuit of understanding the conditioned consciousness to use non-Cartesian concepts, and it is not surprising that his late works share the anti-dualistic flavor of Merleau-Ponty's works. The model of personalization has this flavor about it, for it ratifies a process that includes elements previously bifurcated such as activity and passivity: "The *person*, in effect, is neither completely suffered nor completely constructed" (*FI* II, 6). Totalization is referred to as "the great mixture . . . that aims to surpass them in rigorous unity manufacturing itself as a cosmic determination by being objectified through a hierarchical enterprising whole" (*FI* II, 6). Perhaps Sartre put best this admixture, or ambiguity, of activity and passivity when he remarked in an interview that "every action includes a proportion of habit, of received ideas, of symbols; and then again there is something that comes for our remotest depths and that is related to our primary freedom" (*A*, 352). The image of this model is that of "a snowball constantly increasing in size." Finally, the model of totalization fixes the displacement of the *cogito* begun under the impact of the force of circumstances. We have noted that while "living" a totalization one must think and interpret with the means at hand: "a synthetic activity . . . can comprehend and resolve problems only insofar as it is directed and limited by the concrete totality of the determinations it preserves within it" (*FI* II, 4). While Sartre referred to new experience as "cosmic aggression," it is clear that encounter with the new, the foreign, otherness in general, is beneficial to one's development. The brief discourse on transformation plays down the role of consciousness and reflection, for his study of the conditioned consciousness has led Sartre to conclude that consciousness is limited, has its horizons beyond which, on its own power, it cannot move. It is only by being provoked by the new that one can get a perspective on oneself, on one's presuppositions and categories, that one can initially transform oneself. In this sense, alterity is salvation rather than hell. It is not the force of one's reflective consciousness that controls transformation but a dialogical relationship with alterity which *enables* the possibility of growth.

Our path of entry into Sartre's thought has revealed and emphasized how, with the Genet book, Sartre's thought began to contest itself, producing categories of mediation and continuity in place of rupture and discontinuity. Dominick La Capra is representative of criticism which judges that, after all, nothing has really changed.

> It is not simply a question of finding Sartre's later themes in his early works or his early themes in his later works. It is rather that the more insistent emphasis on certain themes (the importance of society and political commitment, for example) and the use of different terms (such as alienation instead of bad faith, agent instead of subject, or praxis instead of consciousness) do not come with a sufficiently significant change in the structure of Sartre's thought—a change that would imply a more forceful rethinking of his earlier views.[5]

He finds Sartre's thought "repetitious" of the dualism for which, it appears, phenomenology in the culprit. "Sartre's ultraphenomenological view of consciousness as an empty spontaneity inhibits him from explicitly posing as a problem the relation of consciousness and of his own discourse about it to tradition and institution in the largest sense."[6] Certain "submerged tendencies" (counter-tendencies) are admitted to exist in Sartre's writings, but they never surface with enough force to disturb the dominant bifurcations. Thus there may exist a change of theme and terminology, but the substance, as it were, remains the same. My own view is that Sartre's move in the direction of concrete freedom is at odds with the "empty spontaneity" of the early work, bringing him steadily into complicity with the philosophical perspective favored by La Capra himself, that of the human being as "a decentered being who, with more or less critical insight, takes his beginnings and seeks his ends in a historical world where absolute beginnings and ends are ideal constraints or functions of a play of forces that man does not absolutely control."[7] Is it appropriate to depict, as does La Capra, the turn inaugurated by the Genet study resulting in the conceptual moves we have traced out, which have the effect of decentering the *cogito* and embracing a social self, as merely "submerged tendencies"? Admittedly, in each of the works we have examined, Sartre's Cartesianism makes itself present, and his thought contests itself. Moreover, the old ontology, never explicitly renounced, is apparently assumed to be compatible with whatever new concepts and shifts are being deployed. Sartre avoids direct discussion of the consistency of his thought, leaving it, as he put it, to others to determine. For this reason, the remarks he made in interviews not long before his death which do challenge his ontology I consider extremely significant. While what he says does not directly address itself in a detailed way to many of the concepts explored throughout this study, the thrust of what he says is very much in tune with the decentering of the *cogito* and assumption of the social self, and thus offers some corroboration of the view that these positions gained an increasing and then definitive role in his thought.

Occasions on which Sartre explicitly brought up his early ontology were important interviews, given to Michael Sicard and Benny Levy. The interview with Sicard appeared in a special issue of *Obliques* dedicated to Sartre in 1979. Three interviews with Benny Levy appeared in *Le Nouvel Observateur* during the three weeks prior to Sartre's death on April 15, 1980.

Michael Sicard questions Sartre about *Power and Liberty*, the book Sartre is working on with Benny Levy. Sartre depicts it as a morality which "takes ethical problems to their ontological sources." He then states: "This moral investigation compels one to consider the ontology I have developed up to this point as incomplete and false. We wish now to take up ontology anew, in order to understand what a consciousness is, what consciousnesses are originally—an investigation that I have not made up to this time and that we are in the process of undertaking" (*O*, 15). As a result of this new work nothing of *Being and Nothingness* and *Critique of Dialectical Reason* I would be left standing ("mais qui sera obligé de ne plus rien laisser debout de *L'Être et le Néant* et de *Critique de la raison dialectique*"). The new morality will be a morality of the *We*, but Sartre offers an understanding of the *We* as a direct interpenetration of consciousnesses: "ontologically consciousnesses are not isolated, there are levels where they enter into one another . . . there are between consciousnesses interpenetrations" (*O*, 15). He uses an unusual word, "bifide," a two-faceted reality, to express this new position, which does not invoke the mediation of the Third. This new term suggests an acknowledgment of the reality of relationships that goes beyond the dialectical nominalism of *Critique of Dialectical Reason* I.

The Levy interviews focus to a large extent on the theme of fraternity and morality. Sartre criticizes the Marxist view of fraternity, based on relationships of production, as too shallow: "I don't believe the relationship of production is the primary one. . . . If I take society as being the result of a bond among people that's more fundamental than politics, then I take it that people have or should have, or can have, or do have a primary relationship, which is that of fraternity" (*NO*, 412). The fraternal bond among people is "family." Sartre refers warmly to myth and totemism as original expressions of fraternity that have, unfortunately, no meaning for modern man: "I mean that the great concept of the clan, its matrilineal unity—deriving from an animal, for example, that allegedly engendered them all—that's what one must rediscover today, for that was true fraternity" (*NO*, 413).

Myth and totem are invented expressions of a lived and felt fraternity. They express but do not invent the relationship.

> What is not mythological but what is real is, I think, the relationship of you to me and of me to you. . . . The myth is invented by people in the group in order to account for a relationship among them—the group relationship. In other words, they invent—without knowing that they are inventing—a creature that has engendered them all; as a result, they are all brothers. Why? Because originally they felt they were all brothers. Afterward, their invention gave a certain sense *to* this fraternity, but it was not the invention that gave the sense *of* fraternity. It was just the reverse. (*NO*, 413)

Sartre insists on the reality of fraternity because his new morality is to be based not upon a creation of values but upon an obligation to the Other as an already existing value. Marxism defined fraternity in the future, looking upon today's alienated human beings as "submen" to be utilized as means toward the realization of a future value. Sartre recoils from this notion, calling it "absurd." One must recognize the human side that "already exists" in alienated people. The very presence of another human being "constrains" and "obligates" one's actions: "each consciousness seems to me now simultaneously to constitute itself as a consciousness and, at the same time, as the consciousness of the others and as the consciousness for the other. It is this reality—the self considering itself as self for the Other, having a relationship with the Other—that I call moral conscience" (*NO*, 405).[8]

Sartre admits, as he situates his thoughts at present, that he is abandoning the lines of thought of *Being and Nothingness* and of his later Marxism and is now looking "elsewhere." Levy suggests to Sartre: "You're beginning afresh at seventy-five." Indeed, Sartre gives every indication of a conscious decision to challenge, even to repudiate, significant elements of his previous work. He characterizes *Power and Liberty* to Sicard as "a work which completely transforms all that I have thought in philosophy" (*O*, 17). The thrust of his remarks is to de-emphasize and de-center the ontological, epistemological, and moral primacy of the individual consciousness. The human being finds itself already obligated toward the Other, existing in fraternal bonds established at the affective level (with suggestions of an organic or species foundation), which are subsequently expressed symbolically, and entering into real relationships with Others (the *We*) irreducible to external objectification. Hope for the future is found in currently existing seeds of fraternal relationships. The future is not looked upon apocalyptically, but in terms of a further extension of experienced fraternity. While the interviews offer startling assertion instead of detailed argument or evidence of a coherent new ontology, many of Sartre's closest friends were appalled, particularly by the Levy interviews.

At the time of the Levy interviews Sartre was in ill health and had been blind for six years. Levy was an Egyptian Jew with a degree in philosophy from the École Normale Supérieure whom Sartre had met in 1970 in connection with the Marxist publication *La Cause du peuple*. At the time, Levy was using the name Pierre Victor. Sartre had been thinking of renewing his project of developing a morality, this time under the title *Power and Liberty*. When he became blind, Levy was taken on as his secretary; and the project, with Levy's encouragement, was transformed into a transcription of taped conversations between Sartre and Levy. All of those who knew Sartre recognized that the project lifted his spirits, which had been badly stricken by his poor health. Sartre characterized the working relationship as "dialogue," "confrontation," "plural thoughts." Indeed the young Levy by all accounts was treated as an equal by Sartre and assumed an equal stance. Although the interviews were published in the weeks preceding Sartre's death, the dialogue itself had been going on for several years. In fact, these transcribed conversations totaled 800 pages.

When Simone de Beauvoir saw the interviews, about a week prior to the first installment, she tells us "I was horrified," and insists that Sartre's friends "like me . . . were horrified by the nature of the statements extorted from Sartre" (*A*, 119). The publication of the interviews finalized a break between, on the one side, Levy and Arlette Elkaim (Sartre's adopted daughter), and on the other, Simone de Beauvoir and the *Les Temps Modernes* group. The latter considered that Sartre was an old man who was being victimized into betraying the powerful edifice of the work of a lifetime. If my reading of Sartre's journey of thought is sound, however, it should not be at all astonishing that he came to the realization of the inadequacy of his former fundamental categories. Indeed, there is evidence that Sartre was lucid about his action at the time. Jean Daniel, editor of *Le Nouvel Observateur*, relates that Sartre telephoned him prior to the publication of the interviews.

Sartre called me himself. His voice was loud and clear, and he spoke with extreme authority—"I believe you are quite troubled," he said. "My friends must have besieged you. Never mind them. I, Sartre, ask you to publish it in its entirety. If, however, you'd rather not do it, I'll publish it elsewhere; but I would be very grateful to you if you did it. I know my friends have gotten in touch with you, but their reasons for doing so are totally wrong: the itinerary of my thought eludes them all, including Simone de Beauvoir." Seldom had Sartre been as clear, as precise, as much in control of both his thought and his language. Besides, when I called him back to tell him about a minor mistake, and asked him whether he had the text handy, he answered: "I have it right here in my head." And, indeed, he knew it by heart.9

The controversy stirred by the interviews is sure to continue. I am convinced that the soundest way to interpret the interviews as well as to assess Sartre's work as a whole is to be found in his own reflection on experience and thought as totalization in *The Family Idiot*. Sartre's first philosophical totalization was developed upon his encounter with phenomenology. As already noted, Simone de Beauvoir had remarked that until that encounter Sartre's thought lacked "coherent organization." This phenomenological totalization matured into the existential ontology of *Being and Nothingness*. I do not want to imply that there was not an element of stress in Sartre's existential-phenomenological totalization. There are, indeed, scattered texts throughout *Being and Nothingness* that evidence an appreciation for situation and ambiguity. Sartre once depicted *Being and Nothingness* as an attempt to reconcile the influences upon him of both Husserl and Heidegger, a ripe source of tension. It was Husserl who represented the *cogito* tradition and the power of consciousness, while Heidegger's emphasis was upon being-in-the-world. Husserl's influence dominated when Heidegger was chastised for not going through the *cogito*. It was the *cogito*, in turn, which founded the dualistic epistemology of subject/object and ontology of self/other. The dominant discourse and paradigm of this early totalization was the power of consciousness, epitomized by the unconditioned project. Then Sartre experienced the "new" in the form of the force of circumstances. Without any thought about disturbing the unity of his earlier thought, Sartre addressed this new experience, throwing himself into the project wholeheartedly and, in its course, developing new working categories and concepts. These new categories of mediation and ambiguity conflicted with the fundamental categories of his existential ontology, which were exclusory, but Sartre continued to *believe* that his work was a unity and that his earlier categories could assimilate the latter. He appeared to believe this firmly until, after the publication of *The Family Idiot*, he began to make claims to the effect that he wondered how he could have made certain statements about radical freedom, and that he now considered subjectivity and objectivity to be useless notions. The relentless questioning, contesting, and even provocation that went on between Sartre and Levy, particularly on Levy's part, resulted, in my estimation, in Sartre's conscious recognition of the need for retotalization, of the need "to look elsewhere, which is what I am doing now" (*NO,* 400). The interviews catch this point of the recognition of detotalization and tendency toward retotalization. It is noteworthy that, in his remarks to Sicard, Sartre uses the term "transformation" to describe what he is experiencing philosophically: "j'écris un ouvrage qui transforme complètement tout ce que j'ai pensé en philosophie." Transformation is a surpassing unification that conserves. Thus a retotalization will not be a radical creation but a further spiral of development around what Sartre refers to as the "root ideas deriving from his childhood" ("idées-racines, venant de l'infance'; *O*, 21): freedom and contingency. These root ideas, he tells Sicard, must be distinguished from the conceptual frameworks such as phenomenology, Marxism, psycho-analysis, which have served to bind them together into an ensemble that would integrate the archaic and the new. Indeed, it is possible for Sartre to maintain at the same time in the Sicard interview that his new work will "completely transform" all that he has previously written of philosophy *and* that there is a continuous "intellectual unity" in his thought centered about *idées vécues*, which are presented "in a temporal way, at one moment given and then later rediscovered in a slightly (or entirely) different form, but always playing the central role" (*O*, 21). Simone de Beauvoir and the *Les Temps Modernes* group, those Annie Cohen-Solal refers to as "guardians of the Temple, the Sartrian tribunal,"[10] behaved as if Sartre's philosophy was a totality, not an on-going totalization. Perhaps that is why Sartre told Jean Daniel that "the itinerary of my thought eludes them all, including Simone de Beauvoir." It was Sartre, ever open to the new, who by transforming his thought until the end demonstrated in a more powerful way than his books ever did the capacity of a human being to learn and grow, to transform.

The example of Sartre's personal growth, admirable as it may be, must not detract from critical assessment of the intelligible force of the new paradigm of totalization, a task incumbent upon all who would hope to carry on Sartre's philosophical project. It is toward enabling such a possible appropriation of Sartre's work that this present study, aimed at clarifying that project, is hopefully directed. Without attempting to prejudice any future assessment, I think that certain aspects of his later thought, viewed in the light of his enduring commitment to constructing an ethics and a politics, suggest themselves as especially relevant.

The early discourse of the unconditioned project had about it an aura of radicality. The dominant metaphors of "rupture" and "differentiation" fostered concepts of radical critique, unconditioned freedom, and a height-ened, almost solipsistic, sense of individuality, which would have eventuated into a morality and a politics that would celebrate individual freedom. The discourse of totalization, created to make intelligible both freedom and the force of circumstances, has about it a conservative cast. All life, including the psychosomatic form that we are, has a tendency to conserve itself in a form of equilibrium. There is a "global defense" against outside threats to destabilize, a tendency "to prevent the new from jeopardizing that unity." At the same time, the power of critique, which formerly resided in the capacity of individual consciousness (epoché, doubt), has now come to rest in the provocation offered to a totalization by the "new," "foreign," the "other." This was experienced by Sartre, for example, in the development of the "plural thoughts" hammered out in his dialogue with Levy. Transformation, and thus freedom, is possible, but can occur only through an heroic effort of openness toward alterity which counters the tendency toward conservation (just as in the paradigm of the unconditioned project the drive to be necessary had to be resisted). In the new paradigm of totalization, and the morality of the *We* and the politics of fraternity, critique and transformation require a climate of respect for difference, plurality, alterity. Others are required for the growth of the self in a way they were not in his early work. The free individual, the given starting point of his early thought, has come to be viewed in terms of a developmental process involving a complex of relationships and interdependencies. Individual freedom is not denied but its intelligibility is transformed, and its new understanding requires a similar reconsideration of a Sartrean moral/ political project, which now must admit the inevitable and also positive role of others, and social arrangements in particular, in the process of self-constitution. The *cogito* is no guarantee of freedom. The exercise and flourishing of freedom depend upon a unique set of conditions—interpersonal, moral, social, political. If freedom is a goal, these conditions must be specified and cultivated.

Notes

INTRODUCTION

1. "Interview with Jean-Paul Sartre," in *The Philosophy of Jean-Paul Sartre,* ed. Paul Schilpp (La Salle, Illinois: Open Court, 1981), p. 25. The interview, conducted by Michel Rybalka, Oreste Pucciani, and Susan Gruenheck, took place in Sartre's apartment in Montparnasse, May 12 and May 19, 1975.

2. "Sartre's Errors: A Discussion with Raymond' Aron, André Glucksman, Benny Lévy, et al.," tr. G. N. Sink, in *Telos* (Summer 1980), p. 154. Originally appeared in *Libération,* special edition on Sartre, May 1980.

3. Annie Cohen-Solal, *Sartre: A Life,* tr. Anna Cancogni (New York: Pantheon, 1987), p. xiii.

4. Ronald Aronson, *Sartre's Second Critique* (Chicago: University of Chicago Press, 1987), p. ix.

1. SELF

1. Jean-Paul Sartre, *Situations I* (Paris: Gallimard, 1947); "Cartesian Freedom," in *Literary and Philosophical Essays,* tr. Annette Michelson (New York: Collier, 1962), pp. 180–197.

2. Colette Audry, *Sartre et la réalité humaine* (Paris: Seghers, 1966), p. 7.

3. Cohen-Solal, *Sartre: A Life,* p. 68.

4. Simone de Beauvoir, *The Prime of Life,* tr. Peter Green (New York: Lancer, 1971), pp. 161–62.

5. Jean-Paul Sartre, "Merleau-Ponty," in *Situations,* tr. Benita Eisler (New York: Fawcett, 1965), p. 156.

6. Jean-Paul Sartre, "Intentionality: A Fundamental Idea of Husserl's Phenomenology," tr. Joseph Fell, *The Journal of the British Society for Phenomenology* (May 1970), pp. 4–5.

7. Ibid., p. 4.

8. Herbert Spiegelberg, *The Phenomenological Movement,* vol. 2 (The Hague: Martinus Nijhoff, 1980), p. 447.

9. René Descartes, Second Meditation, in *Discourse on Method* and *Meditations on First Philosophy,* tr. Donald Kress (Indianapolis: Hackett, 1980), p. 63.

10. Edmund Husserl, *Cartesian Meditations,* tr. Dorion Cairns (The Hague: Martinus Nijhoff, 1980), p. 33.

11. Sartre, "Intentionality," p. 4.

12. Edmund Husserl, *Ideas Pertaining to a Pure Phenomenology and to a Phenomenological Philosophy,* first book, tr. F. Kersten (The Hague: Martinus Nijhoff, 1983), pp. 57, 59, 61.

13. Ibid., p. 112.

14. I have attempted to apply Francis Jeanson's observation that there is in Sartre's work an "identification between the phenomenological attitude and the ethical attitude" to various aspects of Sartre's thought. See Francis Jeanson, *Sartre and the Problem of Morality,* tr. Robert V. Stone (Bloomington: Indiana University Press, 1980), p. 183. See also Thomas W. Busch, "Sartre's Use of the Reduction: *Being and Nothingness* Reconsidered," in *Jean-Paul Sartre: Contemporary Approaches to His Philosophy,* ed. Hugh Silverman and Frederick Elliston (Pittsburgh: Duquesne University Press, 1980), pp. 17–29; "From Phenomenology to Marxism," *Research in Phenomenology* 2 (1972): 111–20; "Sartre: The Phenomenological Reduction and

Human Relationships," *The Journal of the British Society for Phenomenology* (January 1975), pp. 55–61.

15. Jean Paul Sartre, "Foreword," to R. D. Laing and David Cooper's *Reason and Violence: A Decade of Sartre's Philosophy* (London: Tavistock, 1964), p. 7.

16. Ian Alexander, "The Phenomenological Philosophy in France: An Analysis of Its Themes, Significance and Implications," in *Currents of Thought in French Literature: Essays in Memory of G. T. Claxton* (Oxford: Blackwell, 1966).

17. Edmund Husserl, "Letter to Arnold Metzger," tr. Paul Senft, *Human Context*, vol. IV (1972), pp. 244–49.

18. Ibid., p. 245.

19. Ibid., p. 247.

20. Ibid., p. 245.

21. Edmund Husserl, "Phenomenology as a Rigorous Science," in *Phenomenology and the Crisis of Philosophy*, tr. Quentin Lauer (New York: Harper, 1965), p. 71.

22. Ibid., pp. 72–73.

23. Ibid., p. 78.

24. Ibid., p. 141.

25. Ibid., p. 141–42.

26. Edmund Husserl, *The Crisis of European Sciences and Transcendental Phenomenology*, tr. David Carr (Evanston: Northwestern University Press, 1970), p. 6.

27. Ibid., p. 267.

28. Ibid., p. 376.

29. Ibid., p. 137.

2. SELF/OTHER

1. Sartre, "Merleau-Ponty," p. 161.

2. Sartre extended his critique of Husserl in his novel *Nausea* (1938) by stressing the irreducibility of factual existence. Neither in *Nausea* nor in *Being and Nothingness*, however, does Sartre recognize or appreciate the "structural" dimensions of facticity as cosmic, bodily, historical, social, etc. On the relationship of *Nausea* to Sartre's critique of Husserl, see my *"La Nausée:* A Lover's Quarrel with Husserl," *Research in Phenomenology* 11 (1981): 1–24.

3. Sartre, "Intentionality," p. 4.

4. Edmund Husserl, *Ideas I*, pp. 69–70.

5. Ibid., p. 71.

6. Ibid., p. 81–82.

7. Ibid., p. 83.

8. Aron Gurwitsch, "On the Intentionality of Consciousness," in *Phenomenology: The Philosophy of Edmund Husserl and Its Interpretation*, ed. Joseph Kockelmans (New York: Doubleday, 1967), p. 132.

9. Francis Jeanson evokes Bergson in his discussion of the "tension" between being for-itself and being in-itself. See his *Sartre and the Problem of Mortality*, p. 150. While he does not explicitly mention Bergson, Thomas Flynn characterizes Sartre's ontological dualism as "that of spontaneity and inertia." See Thomas R. Flynn, *Sartre and Marxist Existentialism* (Chicago: University of Chicago Press, 1984), p. 197. Annie Cohen-Solal, in discussing Sartre's eclectic period prior to encountering phenomenology, writes:

> This intense eclecticism, this relentless dilettantism continues till Colonna d' Istria, their unforgettable professor of philosophy—"a cripple terribly shrunken, much smaller than I"—suggests reading *Time and Free Will* as background material for a dissertation on duration. Sartre will never become completely Bergsonian, and yet, during these years of

intellectual gestation, Bergson will indisputably play a crucial, intense, revelatory role: "In Bergson, I immediately found a description of my own psychic life." (*Sartre: A Life,* p. 57).

10. Henri Bergson, *Creative Evolution,* tr. Arthur Mitchell (New York: Modern Library, 1944), pp. 180, 24.
11. "Things are divorced from their names. They are there, grotesque, headstrong, gigantic." Jean-Paul Sartre, *Nausea,* tr. Lloyd Alexander (New York: New Directions, 1964), p. 127.
12. Joseph Fell, *Heidegger and Sartre: An Essay on Being and Place* (New York: Columbia University Press, 1979), p. 80.
13. John Llewelyn, *Beyond Metaphysics: The Hermeneutical Circle in Contemporary Continental Philosophy* (Atlantic Highlands, New Jersey: Humanities Press, Contemporary Studies in Philosophy and the Human Sciences, 1985), p. 50.
14. Jean-Paul Sartre, "Consciousness of Self and Knowledge of Self," Tr. Mary Ellis and M. Lawrence, in *Readings in Existential Phenomenology* (Englewood Cliffs, New Jersey: Prentice-Hall, 1967), p. 142.
15. Sartre does claim that pure reflection is "the original form of reflection" and "that on whose foundation impure reflection appears." Yet, "what is given first in daily life is impure reflection." The problem, however, remains: how do we come to know that we are "totally free," the requirement for flight behavior? See *Being and Nothingness,* pp. 155–59.
16. Jean-Paul Sartre, "Consciousness of Self and Knowledge of Self," p. 140.
17. Ibid., p. 141.
18. "If I am conscious of an object, simultaneously I am implicitly conscious of not being that object. In other words, my very awareness of an object includes a non-reflective realization that the awareness and the object of the awareness are not the same." Hazel Barnes, *Sartre* (New York: Lippincott, 1973), p. 55.

3. THE INTRUSION OF OTHERNESS

1. Mark Poster, *Existential Marxism in Postwar France* (Princeton: Princeton University Press, 1975), p. 196.
2. Wilfried Ver Eecke, "The Look, the Body, and the Other," in *Dialogues in Phenomenology,* ed. Don Ihde and Richard Zaner (The Hague: Martinus Nijhoff, 1975), pp. 224–46; see also his *Saying 'No': Its Meaning in Child Development, Psychoanalysis, Linguistics, and Hegel* (Pittsburgh: Duquesne University Press, 1984).
3. See note 2.
4. Mitchell Aboulafia, *The Mediating Self: Mead, Sartre, and Self Determination* (New Haven: Yale University Press, 1986).
5. After Sartre's death some people who knew him, including Raymond Aron, Benny Levy, and André Glucksman, discussed "Sartre's Errors" and his treatment of Lefort was brought up. Glucksman said: "He was very harshly dealt with." "Sartre's Errors: A Discussion," *Telos* (Summer 1980): 205.
6. Hazel Barnes, *Sartre* p. 175.

4. MEDIATIONS

1. Flynn, *Sartre and Marxist Existentialism,* p. 130.
2. Ibid., p. 106.
3. Ibid., p. 96.
4. Ibid., p. 132.
5. Ibid., p. 132.

6. Ibid.

7. Our interest in *The Family Idiot* is with Sartre's view of the constitutional incapacity of Flaubert, his passive activity. This material continues the probing of childhood begun by the Genet book as well as Sartre's relationship to psychoanalysis. We have seen Sartre create two fundamental conceptual responses to cope with the conditioned consciousness. One of these is the practico-inert, or objective possibilities; the other is the alienation of knowledge, or the development of self-concept. *Critique of Dialectical Reason* I extensively articulated the former. *The Family Idiot* takes up both, but I believe that it is with regard to the latter that it breaks new ground. The third volume of *The Family Idiot* returns to the practico-inert, developing it in an interesting way as "objective mind" in relation to the literary possibilities of Flaubert's time. To understand Flaubert as a singular universal, one would necessarily combine both approaches. For the purposes of this study, which are related to the conceptual, methodological responses on Sartre's part in grappling with the conditioned consciousness, it is with the "psychological" material of the first two volumes that we are concerned.

8. Laing and Cooper, *Reason and Violence*, p. 89.

9. Ibid., p. 90.

10. The translation is that of Hazel Barnes in her *Sartre and Flaubert* (Chicago: University of Chicago Press, 1981), p. 182. The French text is from *L'Idiot de la famille*, livre II, p. 721. Hereafter references to this untranslated second volume will appear as *IF* 2 and page number.

11. Jean-Paul Sartre, *The Emotions: Outline of a Theory*, tr. B. Frechtman (New York: Philosophical Library, 1948). Sartre, in this extract from the manuscript "La Psyché" (which he never published), argues that emotions are not passivities but activities. In accord with his early understanding of intentionality and choice, these activities are conscious and elective by definition.

12. Maurice Merleau-Ponty, *Phenomenology of Perception*, tr. Colin Smith (New York: Humanities Press, 1962), p. 125.

13. Ibid., pp. 162–63.

14. Hazel Barnes, *Sartre*, p. 156.

15. Hazel Barnes, *Sartre and Flaubert*, p. 124.

5. TRANSFORMATION

1. André Gorz, "Jean-Paul Sartre: From Consciousness to Praxis," tr. T. Busch, *Philosophy Today* (Winter 1975), p. 290.

2. Ronald Aronson, *Sartre's Second Critique*, pp. 210–18.

3. Hazel Barnes, *Sartre and Flaubert*, pp. 72–73.

4. Laing and Cooper, *Reason and Violence*, p. 89.

5. Dominick La Capra, *A Preface to Sartre* (Ithaca: Cornell University Press, 1978), p. 39.

6. Ibid., p. 24.

7. Ibid., p. 34.

8. In the English translation of this interview, which appeared in *Dissent* (Fall 1986), the French word "conscience," which can be translated as "consciousness" or "conscience," appears as "conscience." I have taken the liberty of inserting the word "consciousness," except in those instances where it is clearly a case of moral consciousness, or "conscience." I am grateful to Thomas Flynn for his advice in this regard.

9. Cohen-Solal, *Sartre: A Life*, p. 514.

10. Ibid., p. 515.

Bibliography

Aboulafia, Mitchell. *The Mediating Self: Mead, Sartre, and Self-Determination.* New Haven: Yale University Press, 1986.

Anderson, Thomas. *The Foundation and Structure of Sartrean Ethics.* Lawrence, Kansas: Regents Press, 1979.

Aronson, Ronald. *Sartre: Philosophy in the World.* London: New Left Books, 1980.

———. "Sartre's Return to Ontology: *Critique II*, Rethinks the Basis of *L'Être et le Néant.*" *Journal of the History of Ideas* (Winter 1986–87): 99–116.

———. *Sartre's Second Critique.* Chicago: University of Chicago Press, 1987.

Audry, Collette. *Sartre et la realité humaine.* Paris: Seghers, 1966.

Barnes, Hazel. *Sartre.* New York: Lippincott, 1973.

———. *Sartre and Flaubert.* Chicago: University of Chicago Press, 1981.

Burnier, Michel-Antoine. *Choice of Action.* Tr. B. Murchland. New York: Vintage, 1968.

Busch, Thomas. "Sartre's Use of the Reduction: *Being and Nothingness* Reconsidered." In *Jean-Paul Sartre: Contemporary Approaches to His Philosophy,* ed. Hugh Silverman and Frederick Elliston. Pittsburgh: Duquesne University Press, 1980; pp. 17–29.

———. "Sartre: the Phenomenological Reduction and Human Relationships." *Journal of the British Society for Phenomenology* (January 1975): 55–61.

———. "*La Nausée:* A Lover's Quarrel with Husserl." *Research in Phenomenology* XI (1981): 1–24.

Catalano, Joseph. *A Commentary on Jean-Paul Sartre's* Being and Nothingness. New York: Harper and Row, 1974.

———. *A Commentary on Jean-Paul Sartre's* Critique of Dialectical Reason, *vol. 1, Theory of Practical Ensembles.* Chicago: University of Chicago Press, 1986.

Chioti, Pietro. *Sartre and Marxism.* Brighton, England: Harvester Press, 1976.

Cohen-Solal, Annie. *Sartre: A Life.* New York: Pantheon, 1987.

Contat, Michel, and Michel Rybalka. *The Writings of Jean-Paul Sartre,* vol. 1. Tr. R. McCleary. Evanston, Ill.: Northwestern University Press, 1974.

Cranston, Maurice. *The Quintessence of Sartrism.* New York: Harper and Row, 1967.

Cumming, Robert, ed. *The Philosophy of Jean-Paul Sartre.* New York: Random House, 1965.

De Beauvoir, Simone. *The Prime of Life.* Tr. Peter Green. New York: World, Lancer, 1962.

———. *The Ethics of Ambiguity.* Tr. B. Frechtman. New York: Citadel Press, 1964.

———. *Force of Circumstances.* Tr. Richard Howard. New York: Putnam, 1964.

Desan, Wilfred. *The Tragic Finale.* New York: Harper and Row, 1960.

———. *The Marxism of Jean-Paul Sartre.* New York: Doubleday, 1966.

Dreyfus, Hubert, and Piotr Hoffman. "Sartre's Conception of Consciousness: From Lucidity to Opacity." In *The Philosophy of Jean-Paul Sartre.* Ed. P. Schilpp. La Salle, Ill.: Open Court, 1981.

Fell, Joseph. *Heidegger and Sartre: An Essay on Being and Place.* New York: Columbia University Press, 1979.

Flynn, Thomas. "Praxis and Vision: Elements of a Sartrean Epistemology." *The Philosophical Forum* (Fall 1976): 21–43.

———. "An End to Authority: Epistemology and Politics in the Later Sartre." *Man and World* 10 (1977): 448–65.

———. *Sartre and Marxist Existentialism.* Chicago: University of Chicago Press, 1984.

Gervais, Charles. "Y a-t-il un deuxieme Sartre?" *Revue Philosophique de Louvain* (Fevrier 1969): 74–103.

Gorz, André. "Jean-Paul Sartre: From Consciousness to Praxis." Tr. T. Busch. *Philosophy Today* (Winter 1975): 283–86.

Jameson, Fredric. *Marxism and Form*. Princeton: Princeton University Press, 1971.

Jeanson, Francis. *Sartre and the Problem of Morality*. Tr. Robert Stone. Bloomington: Indiana University Press, 1981.

La Capra, Dominick. *A Preface to Sartre*. Ithaca, New York: Cornell University Press, 1978.

Laing, R. D., and D. G. Cooper. *Reason and Violence: A Decade of Sartre's Philosophy, 1950–1960*. London: Tavistock, 1964.

Leland, Dorothy. "A Sartrean *Cogito*: A Journey between Versions." *Research in Phenomenology* (1975): 129–41.

Llewelyn, John. *Beyond Metaphysics? The Hermeneutic Circle in Contemporary Continental Philosophy*. Atlantic Highlands, New Jersey: Humanities Press, 1985.

Manser, Anthony. *Sartre: A Philosophic Study*. New York: Oxford University Press, 1967.

McBride, William. "Jean-Paul Sartre: Man, Freedom, and Praxis." In *Existential Philosophers from Kierkegaard to Merleau-Ponty*," ed. George Schrader. New York: McGraw-Hill, 1967; pp. 261–329.

———. *Social Theory at a Crossroads*. Pittsburgh: Duquesne University Press, 1980.

McMahon, Joseph. *Human Being: The World of Jean-Paul Sartre*. Chicago: University of Chicago Press, 1971.

Merleau-Ponty, Maurice. *Phenomenology of Perception*. Tr. Colin Smith. New York: Humanities Press, 1962.

Mirvish, Adrian. "Sartre and the Gestaltists: Demythologizing (Part of) *Being and Nothingness*." *Journal of the British Society for Phenomenology* (October 1980): 207–224.

———. "Sartre on Perception and the World." *Journal of the British Society for Phenomenology* (May 1983): 118–74.

Morris, Phyllis. *Sartre's Concept of a Person: An Analytic Approach*. Amherst: University of Massachusetts Press, 1976.

Natanson, Maurice. "Phenomenology and Existentialism: Husserl and Sartre on Intentionality." *Modern Schoolman* (November 1959): 1–9.

Poster, Mark. *Existential Marxism in Post-War France: From Sartre to Althusser*. Princeton: Princeton University Press, 1975.

Sartre, Jean-Paul. *Cahiers pour une morale*. Paris: Gallimard, 1983.

———. *Les Carnets de la drôle de la guerre: Novembre 1939–Mars 1940*. Paris: Gallimard, 1983.

———. "Les Communistes et la paix," *Situations II*. Paris: Gallimard, 1964.

———. *Critique de la raison dialectique*, tome I (1960); tome II (1983). Paris: Gallimard.

———. *L'Être et le Néant*. Paris: Gallimard, 1943.

———. *L'Idiot de la famille*, livres I–III. Paris: Gallimard, 1971–72.

———. "La liberté cartésienne," *Situations* I. Paris: Gallimard, 1947.

———. *Les Mots*. Paris: Gallimard, 1963.

———. *La Nausée*. Paris: Gallimard, 1938.

———. *Questions de méthode*. Paris: Gallimard, 1964.

———. *Saint Genet: Comédien et martyr*. Paris: Gallimard, 1952.

———. *La Transcendence de l'ego*. Introduction, notes, and appendixes by Sylvie Le Bon. Paris: Vrin, 1965.

Schilpp, Phillip, ed. *The Philosophy of Jean-Paul Sartre*. La Salle, Ill.: Open Court, 1981.

Sheridan, Jones. *Sartre: The Radical Conversion.* Athens: Ohio University Press, 1969.

Silverman, Hugh. "Sartre and the Structuralists." *International Philosophical Quarterly* (September 1978): 341–58.

Silverman, Hugh, and Fred Elliston, eds. *Jean-Paul Sartre: Contemporary Approaches to His Philosophy.* Pittsburgh: Duquesne University Press, 1980.

Ver Eecke, Wilfried. "Lacan, Sartre, Spitz on the Problem of the Body and Intersubjectivity." *Journal of Psychology* (Fall 1985): 73–76.

———. *Saying 'No': Its Meaning in Child Development, Psychoanalysis, Linguistics, and Hegel.* Pittsburgh: Duquesne University Press, 1984.

Index

Aboulafia, Mitchell, 51, 79
Alexander, Ian, 14
Alienation: of knowledge, 69, 70, 77, 91; social, 52, 63, 69, 90
Aron, Raymond, 2, 3
Audry, Colette, 2

Barnes, Hazel, 58, 84
Being, 18, 26; being-in-the-world, 14, 31, 38, 44, 69; break in, 32, 34; necessary, 32, 35; regions of, 19; unity-as-being, 91. *See also* Existence; For-itself; In-itself; Other
Bergson, Henri, 3; Sartre's criticism of, 26
Body: and constitution, 27–29; for-itself as, 27; objectified, 34
Brunschwicg, Léon: *La conscience occidentale,* 3

Class, 44, 58; and alienation, 52, 54, 69; as a mode of existence, 68; class consciousness, 46, 52–53; as real unity, 55; worker as a transcendence, 69–70
Cogito, 21, 50, 96; and praxis, 86–87; displacement of, 81; pre-reflective, 31, 32, 38, 70, 72; reflective, 5–6; as Sartre's point of departure, 5
Cohen-Solal, Annie, 3, 100
Consciousness: autonomy of, 16; cogitatio, 20; cogitatum, 20; and ego, 6–7, 8–11; immediate, 36–37, 38; individual, 100; intentionality of, 6–8, 14, 19, 23, 25, 29; and negativity, 51, 64; non-positional, 7–8, 66, 86; non-thetic, 37, 81; object of, 20–21; perceptual, 12, 20; phenomenology on, 4, 95; power of, 41, 42, 55, 57, 62–63; pre-reflective, 21, 31, 36–37, 38; reflective, 5–8, 31, 32–33, 36–37, 95; reification of, 5–8, 9, 24; self-consciousness, 66, 81, 86; socially conditioned, 87–88; spontaneity of, 12, 26; and subject, 46; temporal stream of, 25–26; transcendence of, 14; transcendental, 7–9, 9–11; the unconscious, 83
Constitution, 17, 26; and project, 12, 14, 27–29
Cooper, D. G., 79–80, 94
Culture, 17, 66; *epoché* of, 16; and hermeneutic understanding, 38

Daniel, Jean, 98–99, 100
De Beauvoir, Simone, 2, 3, 84, 100; on Levy's interview, 98–99
Descartes, René, 3, 7, 26, 49, 69; cartesianism, 21, 87, 88, 93, 96; his methodical doubt, 1, 7; dualism of, 26; on freedom, 1–2; his influence on Sartre, 2; *res cogitans,* 26; *res extensa,* 26; Sartre's criticism of, 5–6, 9. *See also* Cogito

Ego: and consciousness, 6–7, 8–11; ego-less lived experience, 7–8; egological theory of consciousness, 6–8; and freedom, 7, 9–11
Elkaim, Arlette, 98
Engels, Friedrich, 60
Epistemology, 7, 66; and subject/object relationship, 20–22, 36, 37, 40
Ethics, 14, 40; and fraternity, 96–97; moral conscience, 97; ontological sources of, 96; and responsibility, 71
Existence: absolute, 14, 26, 68; authentic, 11; factical, 26–27. *See also* Being
Existentialism, 77; bourgeois origins of, 61; and cogito, 5; existential stoicism, 14; and freedom, 7, 72; and Marxism, 61; phenomenological, 5; and subject/object relationship, 7; as a theory of production, 60
Experience, 18; concrete, 60; ego-less, 8; interior, 42, 91; lived, 8, 60, 83–84, 85; and social conditioning, 60–61; as ego–less, 8; of totalization of, 92–93, 94–95

Facticity, 80; and being-in-the-world, 31; and contingency, 35; and existence, 26–27; and freedom, 44–45; and project, 28
Fell, Joseph, 29–30
Finitude, 14; human, 40
Flaubert, Gustave; Sartre's study of, 51, 59, 65, 72, 77–89, 94
Flynn, Thomas, 70
For-itself, 18, 27, 36; and facticity, 45; freedom of, 50; as negation of the other, 46; objectification of, 23–24; and reflection, 30; spontaneity of, 23; temporality of, 22–23, 24, 48
Freedom, 12; and alienation, 5, 10, 37, 51, 52, 54, 62–63, 63, 65; and authenticity, 32, 33, 34, 36–37, 48, 72, 84–85; and bad faith, 31–34, 36–37, 48, 72, 81, 84, 90, 93; change in Sartre's concept of, 41–42, 47, 58; and choice, 12, 36, 44; concrete, 62, 81; and ego, 7, 9–11; existentialist theory of, 4, 17; and facticity, 44–45; and good faith, 33; and history, 62–63; human, 1, 48, 49; individual, 100–101; and intentionality, 93–94; and liberation, 51–57; and praxis, 86; radical, 23, 41, 93; and responsibility, 10; and social conditioning, 43–44, 48, 51; total, 44; and transcendence, 10, 31
French Communist Party, 52, 54
Freudism, 59, 63, 73

Lightning Source UK Ltd.
Milton Keynes UK
UKHW020303150919
349775UK00007B/562/P